SHEPHERD'S NOTES
Christian Classics

D1565183

SHEPHERD'S NOTES
Christian Classics

Augustine's Confessions

BROADMAN
&HOLMAN
PUBLISHERS

Nashville, Tennessee

Shepherd's Notes—Augustine's *Confessions*
© 1998
by Broadman & Holman Publishers
Nashville, Tennessee
All rights reserved
Printed in the United States of America

0–8054–9199–6
Dewey Decimal Classification: 270.2
Subject Heading: AUGUSTINE
Library of Congress Card Catalog Number: 98–21267

Library of Congress Cataloging-in-Publication Data

DeVries, Mark.
St. Augustine's Confessions / Mark DeVries, editor [i.e. author].
Kirk Freeman, general editor.
     p. cm. — (Shepherd's notes. Christian classics)
    Includes bibliographical references.
    ISBN 0–8054–9199–6
    1. Augustine, Saint, Bishop of Hippo. Confessions. 2. Augustine, Saint, Bishop of Hippo. I. Freeman, Kirk, 1966–. II. Title. III. Series.
  BR65.A62D48   1998
  270.2'092—dc21
    [b]   98–21267
                                            CIP

1 2 3 4 5 6   03 02 01 00 99 98

CONTENTS

Foreword vi

How to Use This Book vii

Introduction 1

Book I—Early Years 8

Book II—Adolescence 14

Book III—Student at Carthage 19

Book IV—Manichee and Astrologer 26

Book V—Carthage, Rome, and Milan 31

Book VI—Secular Ambitions and Conflicts . 38

Book VII—A Neoplatonic Quest 46

Book VIII—The Birth Pangs of

Conversion 53

Book IX—Cassiciacum: To Monica's

Death 61

Book X—Memory 68

Book XI—Time and Eternity 76

Book XII—Platonic and Christian

Creation 82

Book XIII—Finding the Church in

Genesis 92

Bibliography 101

FOREWORD

Dear Reader:

Shepherd's Notes—Classics Series is designed to give you a quick, step-by-step overview of some of the enduring treasures of the Christian faith. They are designed to be used alongside the classic itself—either in individual study or in a study group.

Classics have staying power. Although they were written in a particular place and time and often in response to situations different than our own, they deal with problems, concerns, and themes that transcend time and place.

The faithful of all generations have found spiritual nourishment in the Scriptures and in the works of Christians from earlier generations. Martin Luther and John Calvin would not have become who they were apart from their reading Augustine. God used the writings of Martin Luther to move John Wesley from a religion of dead works to an experience at Aldersgate in which his "heart was strangely warmed."

It is an awesome sight—these streams of gracious influence flowing from generation to generation.

Shepherd's Notes—Classics Series will help you take the first steps in claiming and drawing strength from your spiritual heritage.

Shepherd's Notes is designed to bridge the gap between now and then and to help you understand, love, and benefit from the company of saints of an earlier time. Each volume gives you an overview of the main themes dealt with by the author and then walks with you step-by-step through the classic.

Enjoy!
In Him,

David R. Shepherd
Editor-in-Chief

DESIGNED FOR THE BUSY USER

Shepherd's Notes for Augustine's *Confessions* is designed to provide an easy-to-use tool for gaining a quick overview of the major themes and the structure of *Confessions*.

Shepherd's Notes are designed for laymen, pastors, teachers, small-group leaders and participants, as well as the classroom student.

DESIGNED FOR QUICK ACCESS

Persons with time restraints will especially appreciate the timesaving features built into *Shepherd's Notes*. All features are designed to work together to aid a quick and profitable encounter with *Confessions*—to point the reader to sections in *Confessions* where they may want to spend more time and go deeper.

Book-at-a-Glance. Confessions is divided into 13 books. Book-at-a-Glance provides a listing of the major sections of that book.

Summary. Each book of *Confessions* is summarized section by section.

Shepherd's Notes—Commentary. Following the summary of the book, a commentary is provided. This enables the reader to look back and see the major themes that make up that particular book.

Icons. Various icons in the margin provide information to help the reader better understand that part of the text. Icons include:

Shepherd's Notes Icon. This icon denotes the commentary section of each book of the *Confessions*.

Scripture Icon. Scripture verses often illuminate passages in *Confessions*.

Historical Background Icon. Many passages in *Confessions* are better understood in the light of historical, cultural, biographical, and geographical information.

Quotes Icon. This icon marks significant quotes from *Confessions* or from other sources that illuminate the *Confessions*.

Points to Ponder Icon. These questions and suggestions for further thought will be especially useful in helping both individuals and groups see the relevance of *Confessions* for our time.

They year 410 ushered in a turbulent and troubled age. Rome, the "Eternal City," had been captured and sacked by the barbarians. Impossible! Unthinkable! Yet sadly true. Marcus Aurelius, for years battling on the frontier, had foreseen the danger as others had. During this crisis, which must have seemed like the end of the world, the church responded with an answer for all time.

Augustine, bishop of an obscure town (Hippo) in North Africa, said the true cause of calamity was to be found in the moral decay of Roman society. The theater, the temples, and the public games reeked with violence and moral sickness. Much to his credit, Augustine was not satisfied with criticism of the evils of the situation in which he found himself. Rather he attempted to frame a Christian worldview, with the hope of reconstructing the very fabric of the civilized world. The reconstruction was the consuming, underlying principle of most of his literary work.

Augustine's extensive writings are still read and discussed by thousands who seek wisdom. He was a passionate writer, as anyone who reads his *Confessions* will see. In this, his most popular work, today's readers respond with personal anguish to Augustine's spiritual struggles, to the throbbing intensity of Augustine's feelings in writing *Confessions*. Many see facets of their own lives in Augustine's story.

His early struggles with Manichaeans and Donatists stimulate present-day debates on the perennial problems of evil and church politics.

Born in North Africa more than 1,644 years ago, he studied rhetoric in Carthage and Rome. As a young man he was attracted to several schools of thought —Manichaeism, skepticism, and Neoplatonism. At age thirty-four he became a Christian and a bishop in 395. Little in his family background would suggest to the historical psychologist that he would become one of the foremost defenders of the Christian faith. In his main works, one finds the nuclei of most of the ethical thought from his time to our own. After forty years of literary productivity, he died in 430.

Donatists

A separatist movement centering around Donatus, bishop of Carthage (d. 347) in fourth-century Africa. Donatists had a high view of the role of the priest in the sacraments and a great respect for every word of Scripture as the Word of God. They considered Christians who had surrendered the Scriptures under persecution to the Romans to be heretics. Donatism grew out of the teachings of Tertullian (c. 155–220) and Cyprian (200–58). Donatists survived until the seventh century.

His exposition of Christian teaching in essays such as *Christian Instruction* and *The Trinity* remain important source documents for contemporary theologians of a variety of viewpoints. His commentary on Genesis raised questions about the origin of the cosmos and on the relation of secular science to religious beliefs—questions still very much alive today. His meditations recorded in (and titled by Erasmus) the *Enarrationes on the Psalms* have been the seeds of countless sermons and works of piety. Next to *Confessions*, Augustine's best known work is the *City of God*, a vast exploration of the meaning of history in all its dimensions. His hundreds of *Letters* and *Sermons* are living witness to the similarities between us and our long-distant forebears.

Some of the more important aspects of Augustine's thought were:

1. God is pure Being—immaterial, eternal, immutable, and a unity. In this view, he was influenced by Plato (427–347 B.C.) and Plotinus (A.D. 205–70).
2. The soul rules the body, and its spiritual condition causes good and evil.
3. Humans have free will, and evil exists because humans choose it.
4. The human soul can take part in the divine ideas of God and His will.
5. God can illuminate the soul.
6. Humans are corrupted by sin and cannot reach God or salvation by themselves.
7. Faith is a gift of God.
8. The gospel must be preached so humans can come to faith.
9. The Trinity is one and the same without distinction.

10. Perhaps more than any other writer, his thought defined the teaching on the Trinity, conditions for waging a just war, and the original sin of Adam and Eve.

Augustine was the source of much that is most characteristic in western Christianity. It would be hard to overestimate his place in history. His works greatly affected Calvin, Luther, and the Reformation.

In 1998, Vernon Bourke, arguably the most famous living Augustine scholar, on the eve of his ninety-first birthday wrote: "More and more I'm realizing that Augustine helped to mold the Christian Church after 400 A.D. He is really the only African writer influential in all later centuries." Incredibly, after Bourke's 66 years of publications: 23 books and monographs, 36 contributions to books, and 77 scholarly articles, he says he is still realizing how influential Augustine has been and is!

The serious student of Augustine will soon realize the importance of chronological order to the understanding of Augustine's thought. One illustration of this lies in the area of human freedom and the workings of divine grace.

In the early philosophical treatises (such as *On Free Choice*) he stressed the role of free will throughout man's moral and religious life. But he spoke very little there about divine grace. Later, as a bishop involved in lengthy discussion with Pelagians and Semi-Pelagians, Augustine emphasized the need for divine help in all that we do. He said we can perform no meritorious acts without the assistance of God's grace. To those who read only the later works, he may appear to be teaching complete predestination of man's decision. But others, who concentrate

Augustine was called the "first modern man" by Adolf Harnack. Pope John Paul II called him the "common father of Christian civilization." *Time* magazine (September 29, 1986), following Jerome, the translator of the Latin Bible, called Augustine "The Second Founder of the Faith."

In the opening chapter of his *Retractiones*, his last review of his writing, Augustine offered his own advice on how to read him: "Whoever will read my little works in the order in which they were written will perhaps discover how much progress I made in writing."

The central theme of longing and satisfaction is commonplace in Greek thought and metaphysics from Plato's *Symposium* onward. While Augustine differs with Plato in many respects, there is a strong relationship between his thought and Greek metaphysical ideas—especially regarding the themes of rest, peace, and fulfillment. Augustine would say that true rest and fulfillment come only in God through Christ.

Confessions has not been without its critics, both ancient and modern. Some have been put off by the sophistication of the style with which Augustine wrote his *Confessions*, in an age in which elegant prose was often more respected than a cogent argument. Others (most notably Pelagius) have been alarmed by Augustine's strong language describing the impotence of the human condition, fearing that readers would rely so entirely on divine grace that moral chaos would result (Chadwick).

on the early writings, will find a champion of personal freedom.

As he opened *Confessions*, Augustine announced the major theme of his work with the words, "You stir man to take pleasure in praising you, because you have made us for yourself, and our heart is restless until it rests in you." This theme of the soul's finding rest in God continues throughout *Confessions*, even to the last chapter of the last book.

Three unique features of *Confessions* strike the reader immediately:

1. Augustine's audience. This is no typical autobiography. Though it is clearly written to be shared with the church, the explicit audience of *Confessions* is not the reader but God Himself. The entire book is written in the form of a prayer.
2. Augustine's dependence on the language of Scripture. In the first book alone, Augustine referred to more than sixty passages from Scripture (more than forty of them from the Psalms).
3. Augustine's apparent disinterest in details. It is notable that in the first book of *Confessions*, we hear nothing about the location of his birth, the names of his parents or teachers, the names of the schools he attended, or the names of his classmates.

BIOGRAPHICAL AND HISTORICAL BACKGROUND

Because the *Confessions* is by nature an autobiography, a lengthy biography in the introduction would be repetitive. Instead the introduction includes a brief outline of Augustine's life, connecting (in approximation) signifi-

cant dates with the particular "books" of the
Confessions that overlap with that time period.

A Biographical Time Line of Augustine of Hippo

354	Birth (November 13) and early years at Thagaste in North Africa (in the northern province of Numidia)	(Book I)
365–9	His schooling at Madaura (twenty miles from Thagaste)	(Book II)
369–70	Augustine's year at home while his father saved money for Augustine's further education in law	(Book II)
370	Augustine's father's conversion	(mentioned in Book IX)
371–4	Augustine's move to Carthage, the second city of the western Roman empire, to complete his education in law	(Book III)
372	Augustine's father's death; birth of Augustine's son, Adeodatus	(Book III)
372	Reading of Cicero's *Hortensius*, which led to an intense search for the truth and a deep interest in philosophy	
373–5	Teaching rhetoric at Thagaste	(Book IV)
376–83	Teaching in Carthage	(Book V)
383	Establishing his own school of rhetoric in Rome	(Book V)
384	Teaching rhetoric in Milan, reading "platonic" books, meeting Ambrose	(Books V–VII)
385	Monica's arrival in Milan	(Book VI)
386–August	Conversion in the garden and travel to Cassiciacum	(Book VIII)
387	(April 24, Holy Saturday) Baptism, along with his friend, Alypius, and his son, Adeodatus	(Book IX)

A BIOGRAPHICAL TIME LINE OF AUGUSTINE OF HIPPO

387	The decision to return to Africa, autumn in Ostia en route to Africa, Monica's death in Ostia	(Book IX)
	End of events recorded in *Confessions*	
388	Returned home to Thagaste (August)	
389	Adeodatus died (at age 17)	
396	Appointed assistant bishop to Valerius	
397	Valerius died and the care of the diocese fell to Augustine	
397–8	The *Confessions* written (397–400)	
400–19	Anti-Donatist writings	
410	Alaric and the Goths sacked Rome	
412–30	Anti-Pelagian writings	
413	Began writing *City of God*	
426	Completed *City of God* (in 22 books)	
430–1	Hippo under siege by the Vandals	
430	August 28, Augustine died in the fourth month of the Vandal attack.	

Augustine wrote to convince others that despite his current saintly reputation, any good qualities he possessed were a result not of his goodness but of the grace of God. Though he certainly had the desire to declare the goodness and grace of God in his own life through *Confessions*, the immediate stimulus for its writing seems to have come from two different sources:

1. Augustine was facing questions from critics who challenged his fitness as an assistant bishop. In addition to being distrusted for his cleverness, Augustine's

opponents within the church also recalled how combative he had been against the church before his conversion. They wondered if the monastic communities, which he was founding, were tainted with the heresies of Manichaean dualism. They had concerns about the questionable exploits of his past and about his baptism in Milan without the support of appropriate letters of recommendation from Africa. In addition to attacks from within the church, the Donatists (who were later to be declared a heretical sect) were in the majority in the churches of Numidia, and especially in Hippo. The Donatists used every criticism they could muster from within the church to discredit Augustine.

Distrust of Augustine is reminiscent of the distrust and fear of Saul of Tarsus when he was converted from being a persecutor of the church to being one of its strongest allies.

2. In 395, Augustine's friend, Alypius (by this time bishop of Thagaste), received a request from Paulinus, a wealthy man who had renounced the world and its wealth, that Alypius send an autobiography explaining how he had come to embrace his current way of life and by what means he came to be baptized and ordained. Alypius shared this request with Augustine. It is hardly coincidental that Book VI of *Confessions* consists of a lengthy biography of Alypius (Chadwick, pp. xii–xiii).

Church Fathers

Also referred to as the Doctors of the Church. St. Ambrose (334–97) whose symbol in Christian art is a beehive or a scourge; St. Jerome (342–430) whose symbol is an inkhorn and a lion; St. Augustine (354–430), whose symbol is usually a heart; St. Gregory (540–604), whose symbols are a cross and a dove. The Eastern Orthodox church venerates St. Athanasius (293–373), St. Gregory of Naziansus (329–89), St. Basil the Great (330–79), and St. John Chrysostom (347–94).

IMPACT OF THE WORK

It is generally accepted that Augustine was the greatest of the early church (or Latin) "fathers" and one of the most influential of all time (Kerr and Mulder, p. 11; NDT, p. 58). He has been described as "the greatest western theologian of ancient times" in addition to being described as "one of the great Christian platonists" (Allen, pp. 82, 102).

His *Confessions* left their mark on the Christian community for centuries and represented a dramatic cultural shift in the way the world was viewed. Cahill's remarks about Augustine and his *Confessions* give the reader some idea of the massive impact of this work:

"We no longer experience the *Confessions* as the earthquake they were felt to be by readers of late antiquity. For Augustine is the first human being to say 'I'—and to mean what we mean today. His *Confessions* are, therefore, the first genuine autobiography in human history" (Cahill, p. 39).

STRUCTURE OF THE WORK

Confessions is divided into thirteen books, which will be referred to by Roman numerals, and chapter divisions, which will be referred to in this guide by Arabic numerals (e.g., the reference "IV:12" will refer to Book IV, chapter 12). Because not all editions of *Confessions* contain paragraph notations, this study has intentionally not included them. All quotations from *Confessions* are taken from the translation by Henry Chadwick (1991), unless otherwise noted.

BOOK I—EARLY YEARS

"But we enjoyed playing games and were punished for them by men who played games themselves. However, grown-up games are known as 'business'" (I:9 Pine-Coffin).

BOOK-AT-A-GLANCE

1–5 Praise, Questions, and Requests

6–7 Infancy

8–20 Boyhood/Early Formal Education

SUMMARY

In the first book of *Confessions*, Augustine related the story of his infancy and boyhood years, speaking both with gratitude for God's provision and gifts to him and repentance for the ways he turned away from God. The book also contains Augustine's biting critique of the educational methods of his boyhood teachers.

I:1–5 Praise, Questions, and Requests. Augustine introduced *Confessions* with a prayer of praise, combining three notable elements: words of worship, questions to God, and requests of God.

I:6–7 Infancy. Augustine described his infancy, acknowledging God's provision in all good things he received. He raised questions about his existence before his birth, affirming that only God is outside of time (foreshadowing his extensive discussion of time and eternity in Book XI). Augustine admitted the sin of his infancy, but, because he remembered his infancy no more than he did his months in his mother's womb, he claimed "no sense of responsibility" for this time that he did not recall.

I:8–20 Boyhood/Early Formal Education. In these sections, Augustine expressed both gratitude for God's gift of life and provision of intelligence and regret for the sins of his boyhood years: laziness in studies, cheating at school, disobeying, and stealing from his parents.

I:8 Language. Augustine developed language skills and subsequently entered "the stormy society of human life" (I:8).

On Questioning God

"Do my questions provoke you to smile at me and bid me simply to acknowledge you and praise you for what I do know?" (I:6).

Family of Origin

Augustine's parents were Monica, his mother, and Patricius, a local government official and small land owner. Patricius was a pagan at the time of Augustine's birth, but his mother was a devout Christian woman. He had a brother, Navigius, and two sisters.

Childish Prayer

"I used to prattle away to you, and though I was small, my devotion was great when I begged you not to let me be beaten at school" (I:9).

Why Delay Baptism?

In Augustine's day, it was traditional in the church for parents to postpone baptism for their children. In fact, because of the intense significance attached to the link between baptism and forgiveness of sins, many delayed their baptism until their deathbeds (as did Augustine's father). Infants, like Augustine, received the sign of the cross, were prayed over for protection, and had salt placed on their tongues. Because of salt's ability to preserve food from decay, it became a symbol representing purity before God. It is in this context that it was put on the tongues of infants in Augustine's day.

I:9 Beginning of Formal Education. Augustine described the "delusions" of success that were set before him by his teachers during these years. He denounced his teachers' method of motivation through beatings. Augustine said that it was in this setting that he first began to pray.

I:10 Distractions. Augustine acknowledged his own disobedience to his teachers and his parents, admitting that he allowed games and public shows to distract him from learning. He considered the inconsistency of adults who are honored for their play ("Public shows are the games of adults.") and who at the same time, beat children who play.

I:11 Baptism Postponed. Augustine told of his early Christian nurture, describing his mother's decision to postpone his baptism. Augustine related that during a serious boyhood illness he appealed to his mother to allow him to be baptized. But before the plans for his baptism could be completed, his health improved, and his mother chose to delay his baptism.

I:12 A Painful Process. Augustine acknowledged his own laziness in learning and his teachers' lack of understanding of education's true purpose, criticizing teachers who seemed to give no consideration to what use he might make of the material he was forced to learn. Nevertheless, God used this distasteful process for good in young Augustine's life.

I:13 Latin and Greek. Augustine reflected on his own education, grateful for learning to read and write and calculate, but disgusted that he allowed himself to weep over stories like Dido's "dying love for Aeneas" while at the same time shedding no tears over his own dying for his "lack of love for . . . God."

I:14 The Difficulty of Greek. Augustine contrasted his hatred of the Greek language, which he was forced to learn, and his love of Latin, which he learned naturally growing up.

I:15 A Prayer for Help. Augustine prayed that God would use all that he had learned in his boyhood in God's service.

I:16 An Obscene Text. Augustine continued his complaint about the foolishness of his own education, referring to a particularly "obscene text." He went on to admit his own sin, remembering the pleasure he took in the obscenity. And he recalled that because of his obscene delight he "was said to be a boy of high promise."

I:17 Style Without Substance. Augustine told of his success in recitation of "empty trifles" at school, condemning the shallowness of this exercise.

I:18 Unworthy Models. Augustine portrayed the superficial irony of writers who are embarrassed not by their obvious sin but by their poor grammar in relating it and who congratulate themselves for describing "their lusts in a rich vocabulary of well constructed prose."

I:19 False Values. Augustine confessed how his own obsession with shallow successes and public eloquence blinded him to his own sin of cheating in order to win. He observed how these small sins have far more serious consequences as we grow older.

I:20 Gratitude. Augustine gave thanks for God's good gifts in his boyhood years: his "delight in the truth," his "good memory," his skill with

Rootless Learnings

"Nevertheless, even during boyhood when there was less reason to fear than during adolescence, I had no love for reading books and hated being forced to study them. Yet pressure was put on me and was good for me. It was not of my own inclination that I did well, for I learnt nothing unless compelled. No one is doing right if he is acting against his will, even when what he is doing is good. Those who put compulsion on me were not doing right either; the good was done to me by you, my God" (I:12).

Something that Matters

"It is true that these studies taught me many useful words, but the same words can be learnt by studying something that matters. . . . This traditional education taught me that Jupiter punishes the wicked with his thunderbolts and yet commits adultery himself. The two roles are quite incompatible" (I:15–16, Pine-Coffin).

Excellence in What?

"Look, Lord God, look with patience as you always do. See the exact care with which the sons of men observe the conventions of letters and syllables received from those who so talked before them. Yet they neglect the eternal contracts of lasting salvation received from you" (I:28).

What would happen to our churches if all decisions were made, all discussions were had in the context of prayer, with leaders not asserting their opinions or jockeying for position, but like children, raising questions to the Master Teacher?

words, his aptitude for friendship. He went on to confess the root of his sin during those years, seeking "pleasure, sublimity, and truth not in God but in his creatures."

COMMENTARY

Beyond Autobiography. Book I begins Augustine's spiritual autobiography. But before he launched into his own story, Augustine made clear that his will not simply be the story of one man's life, even the story of a man's spiritual life. Rather, the entire work was written in the form of a prayer; this is a story told first and foremost to God.

The first five chapters give Augustine's readers a taste of the style of the work, a work that invites his readers into the most private recesses of his soul. Most readers will quickly recall Augustine's admission of his unbridled passion and his blind ambition. Less obvious, but no less profound, is the way he opened the curtain to the inner chambers of his spiritual journey. His spiritual transparency is perhaps most clearly seen out of the corner of the eye, as the reader catches glimpses of Augustine's utter dependence on the two most foundational, most personal spiritual disciplines: prayer and immersion in the Scripture.

The language of *Confessions* is the language of prayer, a vocabulary Augustine likely learned by praying. In the three pages of the first five chapters alone, Augustine made more than twenty-five references to Scripture. It is reasonable to assume that Augustine's familiarity with the language of the Bible grew out of his own disciplines of solitude in studying and memorizing the words of the Bible. Because Augustine never mentioned these disciplines and because these priorities were for Augustine such an inherent part of the air he breathed, the modern reader might easily miss Augustine's utter dependence on these hidden habits of prayer and immersion in the Scripture.

Throughout most of the autobiographical section of the work, Augustine spoke not the language of assertion or certainty; he did not speak the language of an expert. Instead, he spoke before God with humility, asking many questions (almost 20 in the first five chapters), like an eager student before a master teacher.

Original Sin. Though Augustine admitted that he could "recall not a single trace" of his infancy, he chose to begin his autobiography by speaking of his infancy. Combining the tales told him by his parents with his own observations of infants, Augustine gave confirming evidence for his two-pronged understanding of human nature: First, he acknowledged the goodness of God in his birth and God's tender provision for his needs as an infant. But on the other side of the coin, he affirmed that he was born sinful, that even from birth he was in need of God's forgiveness.

Miseducation. Augustine's description of his boyhood years contains a fascinating "confession" of the sins of his teachers. He condemned their fear-inspiring teaching methods, their shallow obsession with success and winning at all costs, and the system that pressured children to excellence at obscure details of grammar and pronunciation but neglected the development of virtue and love for God in those children. Augustine confessed his own

Augustine seemed to recognize that his story was not his story alone; but in a broad sense, it is the story of every Christian. In fact, before the end of the first paragraph, he subtly implied the universal nature of his story with his famous journey-embarking phrase, "You have made us for yourself, and our heart is restless until it rests in you" (I:1).

"Surely I was sinful at birth, sinful from the time my mother conceived me" (Ps. 51:5).

How do the educational method's of Augustine's times compare with the educational process as you experienced it? What do you wish had been different in your own education? What elements of your education are occasions for thanking God?

boyhood sins as well, telling of his cheating to win, his laziness, his blind ambition to succeed, and his search for pleasure not in God but in God's creatures.

In these chapters the reader is exposed to Augustine's early Christian nurture and learns of his early motivation to pray, namely to avoid beatings from his teachers. Augustine's experience with baptism, interestingly, placed him squarely between the traditions of infant baptism and believer's baptism. Though the Roman Catholic Church (of which Monica, Augustine's mother, was a devout member) practiced infant baptism, Augustine was baptized only after he had become a believer.

BOOK II—ADOLESCENCE

"Can anyone unravel this twisted tangle of knots?...But I deserted you, my God. In my youth I wandered away, too far from your sustaining hand, and created of myself a barren waste" (II:10, Pine-Coffin).

BOOK-AT-A-GLANCE

Augustine's Hometown

Augustine was born in Thagaste in (Roman) North Africa, in what is now called Souk-Ahras, in the country of Algeria, less than fifty miles from the coast of the Mediterranean Sea.

1–3 Youthful Lusts

4–10 Reflections on the Pear Tree Theft

SUMMARY

In Book II, Augustine confessed the sins of his youth (in particular, the sins of his sixteenth year when he was obliged to stay home while his father saved money for his son's further schooling): his lusts, sexual exploits, thievery, blindness to his own sin, and his falling under the powerful influence of his idle adolescent companions, searching for amusements.

II:1 Sins of Youth. Augustine explained that the purpose of the confession of his sins was that he might love God more. The sins of youth brought disorder. Reviewing these before God had an integrating effect on Augustine's soul.

II:2 Love Confused with Lust. Augustine described his adolescent lusts as a "whirlpool" sweeping through "precipitous rocks of desire." He questioned his parent's decision not to make arrangements for his marriage during these years, a decision which might have allowed the "stormy waves" of his desire to be finally "broken on the shore of marriage." Augustine acknowledged God's merciful punishment in adding a taste of bitterness to all of his "illicit pleasures." He denounced the shallow priorities of his parents who focused their primary attention on his education rather than on his character.

II:3 Parental Permissiveness. Augustine returned home during his sixteenth year, explaining that, though his father went to sacrificial lengths to send him to school, he gave little thought to his son's "character before [God] . . . so long as [he] possessed a cultured tongue." Augustine recalled his rejection of his mother's warnings about fornication and adultery, warnings he spurned as "womanish advice." He continued his criticism of his parents, recalling how their permissiveness allowed him to wander far into foolish pleasure. He related that he and his young friends enjoyed not simply their sexual exploits but they seemed to find even more pleasure in the admiration those exploits brought them among their peers.

The Fog of Lust

"The bubbling impulses of puberty befogged and obscured my heart so that I could not see the difference between love's serenity and lust's darkness. Confusion of the two things boiled within me" (II:2).

On His Parents

"[My mother] did not think it right to restrict [my passions] to the bounds of married love. This was because she was afraid that the bonds of marriage might be a hindrance to my hopes for the future . . . my hopes of success at my studies. Both my parents were unduly eager for me to learn, my father because he gave next to no thought to you and only shallow thought to me, and my mother because she thought that the usual course of study would certainly not hinder me, but would even help me, in my approach to you" (II:3, Pine-Coffin).

15

II:4 Stealing Pears. Augustine told of stealing pears with a group of his friends, a theft that took place not because the boys wanted to enjoy eating the pears (they actually threw them to the pigs) but simply for the thrill of doing wrong together.

II:5 Sin's Motive. Augustine confessed that both beauty and friendship are from the hand of God but that sin is committed when God's higher goods are abandoned in order to gain these things.

II:6 Sin's Tragic Perversity. Augustine considered why he found such pleasure in the theft of pears he didn't eat, want, or need. Here he described his condition as "a runaway slave fleeing his master and pursuing a shadow."

II:7 Amazing Grace. Augustine gave thanks for God's forgiveness, urging his readers who may not have fallen as far as Augustine, that they should love God no less and should praise God for preventing their fall.

II:8–9 Peer Pressure. Augustine admitted that, had he been alone, he never would have committed theft. He recognized that the motivation for his sin was not in the pears he stole but in the peers with whom he stole them.

II:10 The Wilderness of Youth. Augustine summarized that his adolescence years were years of straying far from God, describing himself as a "region of destitution."

On Peer Pressure

"Friendship can be a dangerous enemy, a seduction of the mind lying just beyond the reach of investigation. Out of a game and a jest came an avid desire to do injury and an appetite to inflict loss on someone else without any motive on my part of personal gain, and no pleasure in settling a score. As soon as the words are spoken 'Let us go and do it', one is ashamed not to be shameless" (II:9).

$\aleph$ COMMENTARY

In Book II, Augustine gave his readers an amazingly contemporary picture of a young man in the throes of adolescence. He wrote passionately (but with obvious "bishopesque" modesty), describing the sexual exploits of his sixteenth year. He explained the paramount role his peers played in his life during these years.

Parents. Like a man in midlife seeking to make sense of his own story, Augustine was able to speak of his parents' faults candidly. He suggested that the incomparable influence of his peers was due, at least in part, to the neglect of his own parents: "The reins were relaxed to allow me to amuse myself. There was no strict discipline to keep me in check" (II:3). Lacking clear, unified guidance and limits from his parents, he was, in fact, left to himself, vulnerable to his peers, having little resistance to the flow of the crowd.

Images of Adolescence. As he described his adolescent exploits, three images are compelling, each drawing on one of the five senses. The first image (one of Augustine's favorites in *Confessions*) draws on the sense of taste, describing the bitterness of sinful pleasure. He explained that no matter how sweet any of his encounters of sinful experiences were, God mercifully mixed a taste of bitterness to each of them so that none of them was ultimately satisfying.

Second, he provided a visual image. Speaking with words appropriate for the twenty-first century, Augustine pictured the adolescent confusion

Carnal Corruptions

"I intend to remind myself of my past foulnesses and carnal corruptions, not because I love them but so that I may love you, my God. It is from love of your love that I make the act of recollection. The recalling of my wicked ways is bitter in my memory, but I do it so that you may be sweet to me, a sweetness touched by no deception, a sweetness serene and content. You gathered me together from the state of disintegration in which I had been fruitlessly divided. I turned from unity in you to be lost in multiplicity" (II:1).

Out of the Fog

"Those who are seriously attempting chastity are more conscious and soon know a great deal more about their own sexuality than anyone else. . . . Virtue—even attempted virtue—brings light; indulgence brings fog"
C.S. Lewis, *Mere Christianity*.

Youthful Lusts

"Flee the evil desires of youth, and pursue righteousness, faith, love and peace, along with those who call on the Lord out of a pure heart" (2 Tim. 2:22).

Companionship?

"A companion of fools suffers harm" (Prov. 13:20).

between lust and love as a fog created by the boiling passions of puberty.

Third, he appealed graphically to the sense of smell, describing his sinful choices as rolling in "dung as if rolling in spices and precious ointments" (II:3).

Sexuality. As sexual sin came to have a greater and greater stronghold on Augustine over the years, it should come as no surprise to Augustine's readers that when he was nearing conversion, the "habit" of sex was a deeply embedded obstacle to his decision. It is worthy of note that in this context, Augustine affirmed, parenthetically, his understanding that God's law limits the practice of "sexual union to acts intended to procreate children" (II:2).

Sin's Essence. The pear tree incident is a classic case study in the power of one's peers to influence behavior. As Augustine recounted his story, he could come up with no logical reason for his thievery. He did not need the pears to feed his family or his appetite. (He had better pears at home.) He had no need for revenge toward the owner of the pear tree. Nor did he particularly want to steal. (He admitted repeatedly that he never would have stolen if he had been alone.) And yet he found himself stealing, for the sheer pleasure of laughter with friends.

Peers. Throughout *Confessions,* friendship remains a consistent theme. It is important to remember that when Augustine finally moved through his conversion experience, his friends played a central role, some in leading him to faith and others following him in conversion. By contrast, here he described his youthful friends, picturing the raw power a peer group can have, a power that led him to say, "Friendship can be a dangerous enemy" (II:9).

BOOK III—STUDENT AT CARTHAGE

In what ways—negative and positive—did peers influence you during your adolescent years? How about parents? In what ways has God used both the negative and positive influences of parents and peers during adolescence to bring you to Him?

"I came to Carthage and all round me hissed cauldron of illicit loves. As yet I had never been in love and I longed to love; and from a subconscious poverty of mind I hated the thought of being less inwardly destitute. I sought an object for my love; I was in love with love, and I hated safety and a path free of snares" (Wisd. 14:11; Ps. 90:3). *"My hunger was eternal, deprived of inward food, that is of you yourself, my God. But that was not the kind of hunger I felt"* (III:1).

BOOK-AT-A-GLANCE

1–3 Searching for Lovers

4–5 Awakened by *Hortensius*; Unimpressed by Scripture

6–10 Deluded by the Manichees

11–12 Nurtured by a Mother's Prayers

SUMMARY

Book III tells of Augustine's life in Carthage. He confessed his two love affairs that began there, the first with the unnamed woman with whom he would live for the next fifteen years and second with the Manichee religion. Here the reader is introduced for the first time to the intensity of Monica's spiritual ambition for her son.

19

Like Sheep

"We all, like sheep, have gone astray, each of us has turned to his own way; and the Lord has laid on him the iniquity of us all" (Isa. 53:6).

The Itch of Sin

"But where the fingers scratch, the skin becomes inflamed. It swells and festers with hideous pus. And the same happened to me. Could this life I lead be called true life, my God?" (III:2, Pine-Coffin).

Rhetoric

In Augustine's day, and for much longer, rhetoric was an area of higher study. It was the art of persuasion; the effective presentation of a case by clear statement and reasoning.

III:1 Looking for Love. Augustine moved to Carthage and described his hunger for something material to love and his subsequent falling in love. He returned to one of his favorite images, thanking God for mixing "much vinegar with that sweetness."

III:2 The Paradox of Pleasure. Augustine told of his love of the theater, particularly his enjoyment of sorrow and tears caused by the stories. Describing himself as the "unhappy sheep who strayed from your flock," he compared his pursuit of a life of pleasure to an "itch" on the skin, "a loathsome mange" (Pine-Coffin).

III:3 The Wreckers. Augustine, with the sparse details of a single sentence, confessed that it was within the church, during worship, that he began to lust after the girl with whom he later started an affair.

In this same section, Augustine confessed his intense ambition to succeed in the study of law and rhetoric and his conceit in his success. He told of a group of popular and spiteful students in his school called the "Wreckers." He neither associated closely with this group nor approved of their methods, but he felt "a perverse sense of shame" for not being like them (Pine-Coffin).

III:4 A Shaft of Light. Augustine's unexamined, pleasure-seeking lifestyle was interrupted at age eighteen by his exposure to Cicero's *Hortensius*, a dialogue that has been lost. Augustine was profoundly affected by this book. He said that this book changed his "affections." It turned his prayers to God and caused him "to have different purposes and desires." Through this book Augustine developed a love of philosophy and a desire to seek true wisdom. This was the beginning of Augustine's lifelong search for wisdom.

Augustine said, "Love of wisdom has the name philosophy in Greek, and that book set me on fire for it." He explained that the only part of Cicero's book that dampened his enthusiasm was "that the name of Christ was not contained in the book," indicating that even by this point the Christian nurture of his mother had made at least a latent impression on Augustine

III:5 Scripture: A First Impression. After being set on the path to search for truth, Augustine began his own investigation of the Scriptures but was unimpressed by them.

III:6 The Manichees. Augustine fell into the fellowship of the Manichees, "men with glib tongues" who set dishes before him "loaded with dazzling fantasies." He confessed, "I gulped down this food, because I thought it was you."

III:7 Manichaean Solutions. Augustine responded to the attractive Manichaean solution to the problem of evil (i.e., evil exists because God is not omnipotent; though He might resist evil, He does not have the power to defeat it). As Augustine explained, he was drawn to the Manichaean solution because he did not understand that "evil is not a true substance at all but the absence of good." He also admitted that he embraced the ideas of the Manichees because he resonated with their critique of the Old Testament, not understanding that God deals with His people in different ways in different ages.

III:8–9 God's Law and Human Customs. Augustine continued his response to the Manichaean critique of the Old Testament and to their claim that many Old Testament heroes were lawbreakers, reaffirming that some acts are acceptable in some circumstances and not in others. He went on to name the three main categories of

The Appeal of Cicero

In *Hortensius,* Cicero taught that "happiness is not found in physical pleasures of luxurious food, drink, and sex, but in a dedication of the mind to the discovery of truth" (Chadwick, xiii–xiv).

The Religion of Mani

Manes or Mani considered himself to be the paraclete and was crucified in Persia in 277. Mani held that the teachings of Christianity were only partly true. The Manichees were radical dualists, believing that the basic elements of reality are Light (good) and Darkness (evil)—forever struggling each against the other. In their view, spirit is good and matter evil. The way of salvation was a highly complex asceticism.

Sin's Three Categories

"For everything in the world—the cravings of sinful man, the lust of his eyes and the boasting of what he has and does—comes not from the Father but from the world" (1 John 2:16).

"The diet of the Manichaean elect, gathered and cooked for them by the Hearers, included certain fruits, the digestion of which was believed to assist in liberating from the body imprisoned particles of divinity. Permitted fruits did not include apples because of Adam's fall" (Chadwick, p. 49).

sin, explaining that the "chief kinds of wickedness" come from "the lust for domination, . . . the lust of the eyes or from sensuality." Augustine affirmed that the real issue for one who claims to follow Christ is obedience, even when an act of obedience may go against the custom of the culture.

III:10 The Lure of Superstitions. Augustine finally identified this false religion with the name Manichee, as he confessed both his derision of God's "holy servants and prophets" and his foolishness in accepting the complex and fanciful dietary codes of the Manichees.

III:11 Monica. Augustine here told of the impact of his mother's prayers. He related how his mother had come to live with him and how God had comforted Monica with a dream in which she was crying over her son's lost soul. A young man "in a halo of splendour" approached her and asked why she was so sorrowful. She explained her sorrow for her son's lost condition. The young man in the vision told her to look carefully, promising that, if she did, she would see that where she was her son was also. And when she looked up, she saw Augustine standing with her. After relating her vision to Augustine, he cleverly attempted to interpret the dream to mean that one day his mother would become a Manichee. Monica, remembering the exact words of the dream, corrected her son, "No! he did not say 'Where he is, you are,' but 'Where you are, he is.'" Augustine confessed that he was much moved by his mother's answer, even though he continued for nearly nine more years in his Manichaean beliefs.

III:12 Tears of Intercession. Augustine related the story of Monica's repeated visits to a bishop, previously a Manichee, whom she hoped could talk her son out of his false beliefs. But the bishop refused, believing that "the novelty of the heresy" would wear off the more Augustine read. But Monica kept pursuing the bishop until one day he responded impatiently, "Leave me and go in peace. It cannot be that the son of these tears should be lost" (Pine-Coffin). She later told her son that she held to these words as if they were a promise from God.

Head of the Class

"I was already top of the class in the rhetor's school, and was pleased with myself for my success and was inflated with conceit" (III:3).

COMMENTARY

Augustine described his search for love with notable modesty, giving only vague allusion to the unnamed woman who was to become his fifteen-year companion. Throughout Book III, he continued with his characteristic lack of details, giving no names and very little information about the people who led him into the Manichean religion. His style here gives a clue that Augustine was more concerned with the history of his journey that took place *within* him than with the details of what happened *to* him. In this regard, his study of friendship frequently gave only the sparsest details about his friends, reflecting instead on the power of those friendships to influence belief and behavior. His description of the "Wreckers" is a fine example. His description of their behavior was quickly related and promptly condemned. Augustine focused instead on his own paradoxical reaction to them, despising their hurtful ways but at the same time feeling a strange desire to be like them, to be a part of them.

Are there persons or groups like the Wreckers that you would verbally condemn but find some of their actions and qualities attractive? If so, why is it important to recognize your mixed reaction?

The Bible. Because the only Bible available to Augustine was the second-century Old Latin

Unimpressed with
Scripture

"To me they seemed
quite unworthy of
comparison with the
stately prose of
Cicero, because I had
too much conceit to
accept their simplicity
and not enough
insight to penetrate
their depths" (III:5).

The Power of
Christian Nurture

"One thing alone put a
brake on my intense
enthusiasm——that
the name of Christ
was not contained in
the book. This name,
by your mercy Lord
(Ps. 24:7), this name
of my Saviour your
Son, my infant heart
had piously drunk in
with my mother's milk,
and at a deep level I
retained the memory.
Any book which
lacked this name,
however well written
or polished or true,
could not entirely grip
me" (III:4).

Bible referred to by Chadwick as "painfully
close to translationese" (Chadwick, p. 40),
Augustine was not attracted to the Scripture in
the passionate way that he was to Cicero.

But despite his lack of interest in Scripture and
his promiscuous lifestyle, Augustine was unable
to shake his belief, apparently instilled in him
by Monica, that no search for truth can be complete without Christ.

The Manichees. Though chapters 6 through 10
continue to be Augustine's "confession," they
also contain much of his polemic against the
Manichee religion. The Manichees claimed to be
Christian, teaching a version of the Trinity that
denied the humanity of Jesus and considered
the Holy Spirit the other self of Mani, the religion's founder who was crucified in Persia in
A.D. 277.

MAJOR CHARACTERISTICS OF THE MANICHAEAN RELIGION

1. Answering the problem of evil: God is good but
   not omnipotent or responsible for the entire
   creation. An evil force opposes God and is
   responsible for the evil in the world.

2. The polarity of good and evil explained through
   complex mythologies.

3. A disgust for the physical body, particularly the
   reproductive system.

4. Two classes for adherents: the *elect* who were
   celibate, practiced a strict vegetarian diet, and
   forbade the drinking of wine; and the *hearers*
   who were allowed to have wives or concubines.
   Hearers prepared the food for the elect.

MAJOR CHARACTERISTICS OF THE MANICHAEAN RELIGION

5. Rejection of the historical reality of the crucifixion of Christ.

6. Acceptance of St. Paul's letters, particularly Romans 7, describing the battle of good and evil within Paul.

Platonism

A system of philosophy based on the thought of Plato (428/7–348/7 B.C.) of Athens. Plato, a student of Socrates (c. 470–399 B.C.) impacted western philosophy and theology more than any other thinker. In the third century, Aristotle (384–22 B.C.), Plato's most famous student, began to exert as formidable an influence in the West as Plato. Plato is famous for his theory of the Forms. Neither physical object nor simply logical symbols, these ultimate Forms have objective existence. The physical world, ever in flux, imperfectly instantiates these Forms. People are born with innate knowledge of the Forms and by questioning—the Socratic method—they come to remember the ultimate knowledge they already possess.

Platonism. These chapters are difficult to grasp without an understanding of the later influence of Platonic philosophies on Augustine's thinking. As Augustine will explain in Book VII, he was not able to let go of his Manichean beliefs as long as he believed that evil existed in a material way. But through the help of the writings of the Platonists, he learned that evil could not truly be said to exist.

The strongest appeal of the Manichaean religion to Augustine was its simple solution to the problem of evil (e.g., How could an all-powerful, all-loving God create a world in which evil exists?). Augustine could simply not reconcile the idea of a good God creating a world that had much that was evil. The Manichaean solution was appealing to him because it maintained a belief in God, while at the same time let God "off the hook," since in this system, God was responsible only for the good parts of creation.

"I did not know that evil is nothing but the removal of good until finally no good remains" (III:7).

Monica. Throughout his autobiography, Augustine alluded to the powerful influence of his mother's intercessory prayers for him, the model of Jesus' message in His parable of the persistent widow (Luke 18:1–8). Augustine gave little theological explanation of how prayer influences God's action, but he repeatedly affirmed that Monica's prayers were, at

Though there are few, if any, official adherents of Manichaeism today, how many contemporary Christians seek a solution for the problem of evil (e.g., "Why do bad things happen to good people?") by imagining either a weak God who is powerless to prevent "bad things" or a "clockmaker" God who is too distant to care?

A Mother's Prayer

"But you sent down your help from above and rescued my soul from the depths of this darkness because my mother, your faithful servant, wept to you for me, shedding more tears for my spiritual death than other mothers shed for the bodily death of a son" (III:11, Pine-Coffin).

least in some sense, the cause of his being rescued by God.

BOOK IV—MANICHEE AND ASTROLOGER

"I lived in misery, like every man whose soul is tethered by the love of things that cannot last and then is agonized to lose them.... I was sick and tired of living and yet afraid to die" (IV:6).

BOOK-AT-A-GLANCE

1–2 The Search for Approval and Love

3 The Fascination with Astrology

4–9 The Death of a Dear Friend

10–12 The Foolishness of Trusting Transient Things

13–14 The Book Revealing the Drive for Human Approval

15–16 The Continued Critique of Manichaeism

SUMMARY

The heart of Book IV contains Augustine's reflections on his own reaction to the death of a close friend. This death becomes the backdrop for Augustine's musing confessions about the foolishness of dependence on temporal things more than the unchangeable God.

IV:1 Seduced and Seducer. Augustine told of his priorities from his nineteenth to his twenty-eighth year, priorities which centered almost exclusively on himself. During these years, he admitted, he focused on winning applause for accomplishments, on enjoying "the follies of public entertainments and unrestrained lusts," and at the same time, on earnestly practicing the Manichee religion, requiring him to prepare carefully prescribed food for the "elect."

IV:2 Living Together. After speaking briefly of his "selling of eloquence," Augustine confessed the sexual affair that began during these years. Though he was faithful to her, he admitted the wide difference between the partnership of marriage and the arrangement of living together which he and his concubine experienced. During these same years, Augustine explained, a soothsayer came to him, offering (for a price) to ensure his victory in a poetry competition. Augustine was repulsed at the idea, but in retrospect he recognized that although he "refused sacrifice to daemons" for success, he continued, apart from the true faith, to sacrifice himself to them.

IV:3 The Fascination with Astrology. Augustine confessed his fascination with astrology at this time, describing the attempts of Vindicianus, a well-respected doctor who had at one time studied to become an astrologer, to convince Augustine of the absurdity of astrology. Though Augustine was intrigued by the doctor's opinions, he did not abandon his astrological practices.

IV:4 Death of a Friend. Augustine told of his return to teach in his hometown, where he reconnected with an unnamed childhood friend, who had now become Augustine's close companion, so close that Augustine wrote, "My soul could not endure to be without him." Augustine confessed turning his friend away from the true faith and toward Manichean

In the Manichaean religion, every meal eaten by the "elect" was understood to be a feeding on the particles of light contained in fruits and other plants. This holy eating was also believed to help attain the forgiveness of sins for the "hearers" (like Augustine) who prepared it.

Living Together

"With her I learnt by direct experience how wide a difference there is between the partnership of marriage entered into for the sake of having a family and the mutual consent of those whose love is a matter of physical sex" (IV:2).

The Hound of Heaven

"You follow close behind the fugitive and recall us to yourself in ways we cannot understand" (IV:4, Pine-Coffin).

All-Consuming Grief

"I carried my lacerated and bloody soul when it was unwilling to be carried by me. I found no place where I could put it down. There was no rest in pleasant groves, nor in games or songs, nor in sweet-scented places, nor in exquisite feasts, nor in the pleasures of the bedroom and bed, nor, finally, in books and poetry . . . all that was not he made me feel sick and was repulsive—except for groaning and tears" (IV:7).

beliefs. After his friend was baptized while unconscious during a serious illness, Augustine began to joke with his recovering friend about the absurdity of his unconscious baptism. But instead of sharing in the laughter, the young man sternly rebuked Augustine, who chose to postpone speaking frankly about his opinions until his friend had recovered. But within a few days, the friend's fever returned and he died, and Augustine was thrown into despair, wanting to put his trust in God but having only a "[Manichee] phantom" for a god. Augustine pointed to God's hand, pursuing the fugitive, drawing him back to God.

IV:5–7 Bittersweet Grief. Augustine described the painful grieving process that eventually led him to return to Carthage to teach, leaving Thagaste without telling his mother.

IV:8–9 Consolation Through Friends. Augustine described how he found restoration in time and friends, confessing that he used these friendships as a substitute for God.

IV:10–12 God Alone. Augustine entreated his own soul (and his readers as well) not to place trust in transient things but in the eternal, unchanging God.

IV:13–14 A Celebrity. Augustine confessed that he had "loved beautiful things of a lower order" (IV:13), referring particularly to his book *On the Beautiful and the Fitting*, which he dedicated to Hierius, a well-respected orator at Rome, whom Augustine had never met. In these sections he admitted his dependence on the attitudes and opinions of others, depending more on human judgment than on the judgment of God. This work was later lost by Augustine.

IV:15 Flawed Reasonings. Augustine admits his shallow understanding that led to his Manichaean beliefs, confessing that he "did not know . . . that evil is not a substance," reflecting the later influence of the Platonists on his thinking. He acknowledged the related error in his understanding of God, clinging to the Manichaean notion God could not have made anything that could fall into error. He explained that, although his book was based on "fictitious physical images," he was, at the same time, straining to hear God's "interior melody."

IV:16 Misuse of Gifts. Augustine confessed the deception of his own intelligence, first questioning the value of learning Aristotle's ten categories and then acknowledging that, although he was quick to learn, he was looking away from the most important things. He concluded this book with a clear rejection of his Manichaean religion and an embracing of God.

COMMENTARY

Friendship. Book IV continues Augustine's (unintentional?) case study on the powerful influence of friendship. As the book begins, Augustine seems unable to speak of his condition in first person singular. Instead, he began this book confessing not simply his own condition but also the condition of his companions: "In public we were cocksure, in private superstitious, and everywhere void and empty" (IV:1, Pine-Coffin). Between the lines, it is clear that these were years in Augustine's life when he defined himself in the plural, living with a group identity more than one chosen by himself alone.

The Manichees on Sin

Because the Manichees believed that the human soul was trapped inside an evil body, they understood that, when a person sinned, it was the evil force within that was sinning, not the true soul itself.

And This Won't Be His Last

At the time of the writing of *Confessions*, Augustine had already written five books against the Manichees.

Substitute Friends

"The greatest source of repair and restoration was the solace of other friends, with whom I loved what I loved as a substitute for you; and this was a vast myth and a long lie" (IV:8).

**Rest and
Restlessness**

"If physical objects
give you pleasure,
praise God for them
and return love to their
Maker....Stand with
him and you will stand
fast. Rest in him and
you will be at rest....
You seek the happy
life in the region of
death; it is not there . .
. . For it is by climbing
up against God that
you have fallen."
(IV:12).

Has God ever used a
friend who is not a
Christian to bring you
closer to Him and
strengthen your faith?

At each significant step along Augustine's
spiritual journey (both its descent and
ascent), his friends played a catalytic role, a
fact repeatedly illustrated in Book IV. His
conversation with Dr. Vindicianus (who is
not named until VII:6) planted the seed for
his future abandonment of astrology. His
friend's sickness and baptism and the acute
pain caused by his surprising death were all
experiences that drew Augustine toward God,
even when, as Augustine described, he himself was fleeing from God.

Grief. He related how other friends helped
restore him to strength and became substitutes
for God as he neared the end of his grieving process. And his reflection on the book that he had
written gives readers an inkling of the depth of
human need for approval and applause.

Augustine did not shy away from acknowledging that his friend's death was a tool in the hand
of God, what he would describe in a future book
as God's "severe mercy." God's mercy is "severe"
because, as Augustine believed, God uses even
the most painful experiences, if necessary, to
draw his children back to Himself. His severity
is "merciful," Augustine affirmed, because it
goes to any lengths, knowing that true life is to
be found in God alone

It is significant that both Book III and Book IV
end with Augustine in a state of twisting and
turning within himself. In III:11, Augustine
reflected on God's apparent slowness to answer
his mother's prayers, "And yet you still left me
to twist and turn in the dark" (Pine-Coffin). And
in the final chapter of Book IV, Augustine
repeatedly asked some form of the question,
"What good did it do me . . . ?" In both cases, he

confessed an acute restlessness that seemed to push him beyond his cocksure intellectual certainty.

How do you evaluate Augustine's view that despair can be a wake-up call, reminding us of the senselessness of placing our trust in things that are temporal, and thus create in us a hunger to find something in which we can place our wholehearted trust?

BOOK V—CARTHAGE, ROME, AND MILAN

"But I had already been taught by you, my God, through wonderful and hidden ways, and I believe what you have taught me because it is true, and none other than you is teacher of the truth, wherever and from whatever source it is manifest. Already I had learnt from you that nothing is true merely because it is eloquently said, nor false because the signs coming from the lips make sounds deficient in a sense of style. Again, a statement is not true because it is enunciated in an unpolished idiom, nor false because the words are splendid" (V:6).

Is inner turmoil an important and necessary step for some people as they move toward faith in Christ? Can a ministry that focuses on therapeutically relieving the pain and turmoil of its people at times hinder the conversion process?

BOOK-AT-A-GLANCE

1–2 Introductory Words of Praise

3–7 Conversations with Faustus

8–9 Travel to and Teaching in Rome

10–11 Growing Discomfort with Manichean Beliefs

12 Motivation to Leave Rome

13–14 Conversations with Ambrose

SUMMARY

Alongside the story of Augustine's journeys to various teaching positions (first in Carthage, next in Rome, and finally in Milan), he related his spiritual journey from Manichaeism to a tentative acceptance of the views of the skeptic

Running from God

"The unjust stumble over you and are chastised. Endeavoring to withdraw themselves from your gentleness, they stumble on your equity and fall into your anger" (V:2).

God Can Use a Liberal Education

"I did not notice any rational account of solstices and equinoxes or eclipses of luminaries nor anything resembling what I had learnt in the books of secular wisdom. Yet I was ordered to believe Mani. But he was not in agreement with the rational explanations which I had verified by calculation and had observed with my own eyes" (V:3).

philosophers to an open stance toward the Catholic faith.

V:1–2 Amazing Grace. Lacing these chapters with a preponderance of allusions to Scripture, Augustine praised God for His mercy in making Himself known even to those who have run from God.

V:3 Faustus, the Manichee. Augustine told of his encounter in his twenty-ninth year (while still living in Carthage) with Faustus, a Manichee bishop, renowned for mastery of the liberal arts. Prior to this long-awaited meeting, Augustine had become very familiar with the calculations of those who had learned to predict accurately the movement of the sun and the stars. He hoped that Faustus could resolve the significant contradictions between those calculations and the cosmic mythology of the Manichees.

Augustine laced his reflections with his strong conviction that, though he was aided in his journey from error by secular wisdom, such wisdom can become a stumbling block to the most eternal things.

V:4 Limitations of Science. Augustine made clear that learning, though valuable, is worthless without the knowledge of God.

V:5 Limitations of Manichaeism. Though Augustine sharply criticized the folly of Mani, who wrote and taught on matters that he did not understand (and attributed those teachings to himself as though he were divine), Augustine still left open the possibility that there might be some way to reconcile the teachings of science with the explanations of Mani.

V:6 Disillusionment. Augustine went on to enumerate his disappointment with Faustus. He was not surprised to discover that Faustus was an eloquent speaker, but Augustine quickly recognized that the depth of Faustus' learning was limited to grammar and literature. Augustine described the process through which he recognized the shallowness of Faustus' understanding. First, he was not allowed to ask Faustus questions in a public assembly; and second, Faustus' discipline of learning was limited to practicing his delivery and focusing exclusively on *how* he communicated rather than on *what* he had to say. Augustine acknowledged that, through his conversations with Faustus, God was holding a mirror up for Augustine to see himself, a man who was an expert at rhetoric but who was steeped in error. Also in this chapter, Augustine took the opportunity to make a tangential response to his own contemporary critics who seemed to question his own motives and veracity, assuming that, since Augustine spoke well, he must not be speaking the truth.

V:7 Source of Liberation. Augustine spoke well of Faustus' "controlled modesty of mind," which prevented him from speaking about things of which he knew nothing. But by this time, Augustine explained, he had resigned himself to the fact that Faustus did not have the answers he was seeking. Though Augustine continued to enjoy the company of Faustus, particularly in discussions of literature, Augustine's enthusiasm for Manichaeism was severely diminished.

He admitted that, even though he could no longer hold enthusiastically to the Manichee beliefs, he chose to remain a Manichee because of a lack of other options. Augustine discerned God's providence, using Faustus, who had been a "snare of death" to so many, to become the source of Augustine's liberation.

Total Eclipse of the Heart

"Their irreligious pride makes them withdraw from you and eclipse your great light from reaching themselves. They can foresee a future eclipse of the sun, but do not perceive their own eclipse in the present. . . . They have not known this by which they may descend from themselves to him and through him ascend to him" (V:3).

Unanswered Prayer

How would believers' attitudes toward prayer be different if they understood the principle that God often rejects their requests in order to give them what they truly desire?

V:8 From Carthage to Rome. Augustine continued on the theme of God's "profoundly mysterious providence," this time describing God's secret hand in Augustine's move from Carthage to Rome, with God using disruptive students in Carthage and an attractive offer through Manichaean connections in Rome. Augustine portrayed the acute pain of his mother when she learned of his anticipated departure from Carthage, where she had come to join him. Augustine admitted his shame in deceiving his prayerful mother to prevent her accompanying him on the journey to Rome. He explained that while she was spending the night at the shrine of St. Cyprian, he secretly departed. Augustine concluded this chapter, reflecting on the cause of his devout mother's unanswered prayers, admitting that God denied her request to keep her son in Carthage in order to give her what she most desired, namely the conversion of her son.

V:9 God's Mercy in Sickness. Augustine told of the illness which overtook him soon after he arrived in Rome. He acknowledged that, if he had died during this sickness, he was "on the way to the underworld." He explained that, as a Manichee, he did not believe that Christ's human death was real, declaring with certainty to God, "You had not yet forgiven me in Christ." Augustine explained that, though he "still remained sick in [his] sacrilegious heart," his body was healed, due in large part, Augustine confessed, to the prayers of his mother.

V:10–11 Learning from the Academics. Augustine gave his readers a somewhat complicated interior tour of his thinking as he was growing increasingly skeptical of his Manichaean religion but, at the same time, found himself clinging to those beliefs. He gave a variety of reasons he found such difficulty in abandoning his Manichaean beliefs altogether: (1) He found comfort in explaining his sin as the result of an "alien nature" within him. (2) He was surrounded by a large number of Manichees living secretly in Rome. (3) He could not imagine God without seeing God as a "physical mass." (4) He refused to believe that God could have created evil. (5) His understanding of God left no room for the Incarnation, believing that being literally "in the flesh" would have defiled Jesus. (6) He still had no explanation for the traditional Manichee criticisms of the Scripture.

Though Augustine was still in close association with the Manichees in Rome, he had by this time given up any aspirations of moving higher up in the religion (from being a "hearer" to being one of the "elect"). Hanging on to his Manichaean religion simply because he could "find nothing better," he began to become interested in the teachings of the "Academics," skeptical philosophers who asserted that "everything is a matter of doubt, and that an understanding of truth lies beyond human capacity." He explained that during this time, he began openly warning his Manichaean host not to put "excessive trust in the fabulous matters of which the Manichee books are full" (V:10).

V:12 Rascals. Augustine railed against dishonest students in Rome who had developed schemes to cheat their teachers out of their agreed-upon fees.

V:13 From Rome to Milan. Augustine acknowledged God's hand in his moving to Milan to teach rhetoric, again using Augustine's Manichee contacts to secure the new teaching

Just in Case

"But to these philosophers, who were without Christ's saving name, I altogether refused to entrust the healing of my soul's sickness. I therefore decided for the time being to be a catechumen in the Catholic Church, . . . until some clear light should come by which I could direct my course" (V:14).

"Total Suspense of Judgement"

How would the evangelism efforts of Christian churches be different if their strategies provided for a time of total "suspense of judgement," while God completed the work of conversion?

position. In Milan, he was first exposed to the renowned bishop Ambrose, whom he described as one whose "eloquence valiantly ministered . . . the sober intoxication of your wine." Augustine described his warm reception by Ambrose, comparing his depth and clarity to the empty eloquence of Faustus.

V:14 Encounter with Ambrose. Though Augustine admitted that he had little interest in the content of Ambrose's teaching, his exposure to the preaching of Ambrose soon began to deteriorate Augustine's defenses against the Catholic faith, as he heard the Old Testament Scriptures figuratively interpreted. After his initial exposure to Ambrose, Augustine no longer perceived the Catholic faith as "defeated," but neither did he see it as "the conqueror."

Augustine ended this book in a state of "total suspense of judgement," having decided to leave the Manichees. Considering seriously the input of both the skeptical philosophers and of Ambrose, Augustine decided to become a catechumen in the Catholic Church.

 COMMENTARY

Providence. Book V focuses the reader's attention on the mysterious, surprising providence of God. Augustine confessed that God used Faustus, the most erudite, well-respected Manichee, to lead Augustine away from his Manichaean beliefs. God used Augustine's secular wisdom to free him from his spiritual blindness. God used the destructiveness of pupils in Carthage and Augustine's deceptiveness toward his mother to move him to Rome. God denied the request of his devoted servant,

Monica, in order to give her what she truly desired. God used cheating, dishonest students in Rome to move Augustine toward Milan, providing through them "the pricks which made [him] tear [him]self away from Carthage" (V:8). God even used Augustine's Manichaean contacts to lead him to Milan, where he moved out of the circle of influence of the Manichees.

Style and Substance. The book also gives a fascinating study of Augustine's own wrestling with style over substance. In Faustus, Augustine saw a picture of his own shallow obsession with sounding good while at the same time being hopelessly trapped in error and confusion.

The reader also has a glimpse into Augustine's sensitivity to his own critics in this matter. It seems clear that some were questioning the genuineness of Bishop Augustine's commitment to Christ because he spoke with such eloquence. But Augustine made the case that eloquence or simplicity, in and of itself, does not determine the truth of a belief, and he challenged those who foolishly reject his message because it comes in a beautiful container.

Monica's Prayers. But likely, the most compelling insight in Book V is Augustine's reflection on his mother's unanswered prayer on his behalf (V:8). Her years of prayer for her son and God's apparent slowness to respond can be a corrective case study to an age of consumer Christianity that offers a shallow picture of a small God. Admittedly, throughout *Confessions*, Augustine pointed to the immense impact of his mother's prayers on his behalf, but he did so in such a way that left room for God's mysterious wisdom and providence.

Consider Monica's intercessions for Augustine. Has God ever denied a specific request you've made in order to give you what you truly desired? What can be learned about intercessory prayer by looking at Monica's practice of it.

Style Is Not Enough

"But my thirst was not to be satisfied in this way, however precious the cup and however exquisite the man who served it" (V:6, Pine-Coffin).

Monica's Prayers

"She suffered greater pains in my spiritual pregnancy than when she bore me in the flesh . . . . Lord, of course you were there and were hearing her petition . . . . For your mercy is for ever, and you deign to make yourself a debtor obliged by your promises to those to whom you forgive all debts" (V:9).

On Ambrose

"I was led to him by you, unaware that through him, in full awareness, I might be led to you. That 'man of God' (2 Kings 1:9) received me like a father and expressed pleasure at my coming with a kindness most fitting in a bishop. I began to like him, at first indeed not as a teacher of the truth, for I had absolutely no confidence in your Church, but as a human being who was kind to me" (V:13).

Book V comes to a climax in the final chapters when Augustine finds himself under the powerful influence of Bishop Ambrose.

Book VI—Secular Ambitions and Conflicts

"He did not say anything that I felt to be a difficulty; but whether what he said was true I still did not know. Fearing a precipitate plunge, I kept my heart from giving assent, and in that state of suspended judgement I was suffering a worse death. I wanted to be as certain about things I could not see as I am certain that seven and three are ten" (VI:4).

BOOK-AT-A-GLANCE

1–2 Praise for Monica

3–5 Changing Attitude Toward the Catholic Faith

6 The Milan Beggar

7–10 The Spiritual Biography of Alypius (with a footnote on Nebridius)

11 Winds of Indecision

12–16 Questions of Marriage and Sex

SUMMARY

Augustine continued his description of his incremental steps toward embracing the Christian faith. Through the preaching of Ambrose, Augustine's resistance was broken down. Through his friendship with other seekers, he set his course toward the truth wherever that might lead. But he found himself vacillating, unable to make a decision for or against the Christian faith.

VI:1 Monica in Milan. Augustine told of Monica's arrival in Milan, praising her comforting influence that extended even to the ship's crew on the hazardous journey to Milan. He praised her faithful prayers and recalled her complete confidence that he would become a baptized Catholic believer before her death. Augustine explained that though Monica was delighted with Bishop Ambrose, her response to his departure from Manichaeism was much less enthusiastic than he expected. He related as well that he was in a "dangerous state of depression" when she arrived.

VI:2 Monica's Respect for Ambrose. Augustine told of Monica's custom of bringing cakes and bread and wine to the shrines of the saints, a custom which was forbidden in Milan in order to "avert any pretext of intoxication." Though she immediately obeyed, Augustine admitted that she would have been much more resistant if the ban had come from someone other than Ambrose.

VI:3 Ambrose—in Heavy Demand. Augustine related that despite the fact that the bishop's popularity prevented Augustine from asking his many questions and telling his own story, his opinions about the church were going through a dramatic transformation.

VI:4 The Old Testament Clarified. Augustine admitted that his opinion of the Catholic faith "was being turned around," recalling his delight in Ambrose's spiritual interpretation of the Old Testament texts which had previously been a major source of doubt for Augustine. But having just abandoned the error of the Manichees, Augustine was hesitant to give assent too quickly.

"If you abide in My word, then you are truly disciples of Mine; and you shall know the truth, and the truth shall make you free" (John 8:31–32, NASB).

Rejecting a Caricature of Christianity

"I had been barking for years not against the Catholic faith but against mental figments of physical images. My rashness and impiety lay in the fact that what I ought to have verified by investigation I had simply asserted as an accusation" (VI:3).

VI:5 Intellectual Conversion. Augustine admitted that by this time he had given his "preference to the Catholic faith." He criticized the hypocrisy of the Manichees who mock "mere belief" and then require their adherents to believe "many fabulous and absurd myths impossible to prove true." After considering the many things he believed exclusively on the basis of being told those things by someone trustworthy (e.g., history, places he had never seen, the identity of his parents), he told of his recognition that none of his intellectual questions now prevented him from believing. But still he was unable to commit.

VI:6 Insight from a Beggar. Augustine described his growing recognition that his chasing after success was not bringing him the happiness he desired. His condition was made acutely plain, as he was about to deliver a speech on the emperor, a speech in which he knew he would tell "numerous lies." As he was anxiously on the way to deliver the speech, he passed a beggar, whose condition became a cause of self-evaluation for Augustine. He admitted that his only goal had been to live a life of "carefree cheerfulness," and he recognized that the beggar had already achieved this state, while the ambitious Augustine was "racked with anxiety."

VI:7 Alypius. The reader is introduced to Alypius and Nebridius, Augustine's companions in Milan, giving particular attention in the next few chapters to the story of Alypius, who was later to become the bishop of Thagaste. Augustine recalled his teaching of Alypius both in Thagaste and Carthage, particularly remembering how the "whirlpool of Carthaginian morals" pulled Alypius "into the folly of the circus games." Pointing again to God's mysterious hand,

Augustine recalled how, in one of his lectures, God used Augustine's "bitingly sarcastic" comment about those in bondage to circus games, a comment which caused Alypius immediately to "jump . . . out of the deep pit in which he was sinking." Alypius subsequently joined Augustine in his "Manichee superstition" in Carthage.

VI:8 Obsession with Games. Augustine described Alypius' obsession with the gladiatorial games in Rome, where he had come to practice law before Augustine's arrival there. When Alypius initially resisted his friends' invitation to the games, they used "friendly violence" to get him into the amphitheater. Augustine described the fall of his friend into obsession with these games, concluding the chapter with praise for God's future deliverance.

VI:9 Alypius' Arrest. Augustine related the story of Alypius' false arrest in Rome, suggesting that God allowed this experience to prepare Alypius for the "weighty responsibilities" he would later face as a bishop, a role where he would need to be "on . . . guard against hasty credulity in condemning a man."

VI:10 Alypius' Integrity. Augustine explained that, when he reconnected with Alypius in Rome, his friend "attached himself to [Augustine] with the strongest bond," choosing to follow Augustine to Milan. Augustine praised Alypius' integrity in refusing to take bribes, choosing integrity over expediency, and being "faithful in the little things." Augustine also related part of the story of his other companion, Nebridius, who came from Carthage to Milan with "burning enthusiasm for the truth and for wisdom." Augustine concluded the chapter with his familiar affirmation that God always

Gladiatorial Games

The gladiatorial shows were an integral part of Roman society. These contests were held from dawn to dusk. The main feature was the contest to the death between trained fighters. Also, criminals of all ages and both sexes were sent into the arena without weapons to face wild animals which would tear them to pieces. Numerous kinds of animal contests were also held, such as bears against buffaloes.

brought a little bitterness to all the worldly activities of these three friends.

VI:11 Continued Indecision. This chapter portrays the vacillating mind of Augustine (and his companions) as they searched for truth. Augustine recalled his frustration that at thirty years old, he remained stuck in the same uncertainty he experienced at nineteen. He remembered his frustration at having no time with Ambrose, no time for reading, no clear path for finding the truth, choosing impulsively to put aside all other concerns and focus exclusively on the "investigation of the truth." And in the next breath he hesitated, remembering the sweetness of worldly success. And so he remained in the land of indecision, distracting himself with thoughts of marrying a wealthy woman to boost his secular ambitions, certain of his misery if he "were deprived of the embraces of a woman."

VI:12 Alypius' Counsel Regarding Marriage. Augustine contrasted his own views on marriage and sex with those of Alypius, who discouraged Augustine from considering marriage, believing it would interrupt their longed-for life of "carefree leisure for the love of wisdom." Augustine explained that Alypius had experienced a particularly unpleasant sexual encounter early in his adolescence that left him with a complete revulsion for sex, while Augustine, on the other hand, found himself "stuck fast in the glue of this pleasure." But because of his respect of Augustine, Alypius began to desire marriage for himself.

VI:13 Monica Seeks to Arrange Marriage. Augustine explained how his mother's efforts brought about the arrangement of a girl for him to marry. Though Monica had prayed for a confirming vision from God to give her hope that her son would one day be saved from the chains of sin through his coming marriage, God never granted such a vision. Augustine gave a fascinating description of how his mother was able to discern between true and false visions "by a certain smell indescribable in words." Augustine's mother continued her encouragement for Augustine's marriage as he waited for his promised bride to reach the legal marrying age of twelve.

In Augustine's age it was common belief that evil spirits caused an unpleasant odor.

VI:14 Dream of a Contemplative Community. Augustine and his friends considered establishing a contemplative community, with all the members sharing a common purse—a plan made realistic by the enthusiastic involvement of a wealthy friend from Augustine's hometown. But the group "returned to sighs and groans and careers" when they considered that the plan would never be acceptable to the wives of those who were married or were preparing to be.

VI:15 Common-Law Wife Dismissed. With the sparsest of specific details, Augustine described his painful parting with the woman with whom he had been living for fifteen years, having recognized that her presence would have been a hindrance to his upcoming marriage. Although the woman left, Augustine's son whom she bore remained with him. Augustine confessed that he quickly procured another woman in order that his sexual "habit would be guarded and fostered until [he] came to the kingdom of marriage." But he recalled that the pain of his concubine's departure left him in a "frigid but desperate" condition.

VI:16 Restlessness. Augustine concluded Book VI (as he had the two previous books) tossing and turning in his restlessness without God, although he avoided an "even deeper whirlpool of erotic indulgence" because of his fears of God's judgment. He described his restless soul, as it "turned this way and that, on its back, on its side, on its stomach, all positions are uncomfortable."

COMMENTARY

Monica's Influence. Whether physically or psychologically, Monica remained a constant presence in Augustine's life. Having been a widow for thirteen years and having been away from her son for about two years, Augustine's mother traveled from North Africa to Milan, arriving with the single-minded intent to give her son the full benefit of her influence. When she arrived in Milan, she was not satisfied simply to hear that her son had abandoned his Manichaean beliefs. (Augustine recalled feeling some disappointment at her lack of enthusiasm over this change.) Instead, she was intent on moving him forward both in his faith and in his career, being delighted in Augustine's exposure to Ambrose and arranging for her thirty-plus-year-old son to marry a girl who was not yet twelve.

What positive effect did skeptics have on Augustine's conversion to Christian faith? What are some of the values of skepticism? What are the limitations of skepticism?

Skeptics. G. K. Chesterton wrote, "Tell me about the God you don't believe in, and chances are, I don't believe in him either." Most who reject the claims of the gospel, like Augustine, reject not Christianity itself but only a fictitious caricature, a straw man that is easily knocked down. Augustine admitted that his error lay in the fact that he summarily dismissed the Christian faith before he had fully investigated it.

Friendship. In this book, Augustine also told of the blessing of companions who shared both his restlessness and his voracious appetite for gaining wisdom. There is fascinating irony in the fact that God seemed frequently to use godless people to lead Augustine to conversion. With Monica's relentless presence and Ambrose's preaching as a backdrop, God provided friends who were just as lost as Augustine to move him forward on his journey of faith.

As suggested in the Introduction, it is likely that one of the motivating factors behind the writing of *Confessions* may have been a request for Bishop Alypius to write the story of his own conversion. Whether Alypius ever wrote his own story, Augustine was able to fortify the story of his own spiritual odyssey by recounting the tale of Alypius' journey to faith.

Biblical Interpretation. Ambrose's spiritual interpretations of many Old Testament texts freed Augustine from the stumbling block of his literal understanding.

It is clear from the language of *Confessions* that Augustine was deeply dependent on the Scripture as the unique and final authority for the Christian. Yet he seemed to view the figurative interpretation as somehow higher than a mere literal one. Augstine's infatuation with figurative interpretations of Scripture moved to elaborate proportions in the final chapter of *Confessions* were he offered a lengthy allegorical interpretation of the Genesis account of Creation.

Seeking Friends

"Like me, [Nebridius] sighed, and like me he vacillated, ardent in his quest for the happy life and a most acute investigator of very difficult questions . . . so there were the mouths of three hungry people [Augustine, Alypius and Nebridius]" (VI:10).

Interpreting Scripture

"Those texts which, taken literally, seemed to contain perverse teaching [Ambrose] would expound spiritually, removing the mystical veil" (VI:4).

"The authority of the
Bible seemed the
more to be venerated
and more worthy of a
holy faith on the
ground that it was
open to everyone to
read, while keeping
the dignity of its secret
meaning for a
profounder
interpretation" (VI:5).

BOOK VII—A NEOPLATONIC QUEST

"I searched for the origin of evil, but I searched in a flawed way and did not see the flaw in my search" (VII:5).

BOOK-AT-A-GLANCE

1–8 The Quest for the Origin of Evil

9–16 The Books of the Platonists

17–21 The Goads to Certainty

SUMMARY

Augustine revealed his inner, mental journey, a journey that is likely quite unfamiliar to modern readers. He described his journey away from seeing God as an infinite "mass," to wrestling to resolve the question of the origin of evil. Since laying aside his Manichaean beliefs, Augustine had endured the pain of psychological conflict resulting from his holding logically incompatible beliefs. He found resolution through the books of the Platonists. Though he clearly desired to embrace the faith of the church, still he hesitated, recalling his past naivete in too quickly accepting the Manichaean beliefs.

VII:1–2 Revisioning God. Augustine revealed his relentless quest to see God with a new understanding, one that did not limit God to a physical perception, acknowledging that according to his limited understanding of God at this time, ". . . more of [God] would be contained by an elephant's body than a sparrow's" (VII:1).

VII:3 Continued Perplexity. Augustine admitted that although by this time he had become fully convinced that his previously held Manichaean ideas were false, he still could not resolve the question of the origin of evil, a situation that "depressed" and "suffocated" him.

VII:4 Highest Good. Augustine affirmed the absolute incorruptibility of God and His supreme power and knowledge.

VII:5 Flawed Understanding. Augustine admitted a fundamental flaw in the way he was searching for a solution to the origin of evil, namely his limited, physical understanding of God. Augustine explained that he understood God as an infinite sea and the Creation as a massive but finite sponge. This understanding left no room to explain how evil crept in. He concluded this chapter, explaining that his "gnawing cares" left his faith "still unformed and hesitant." Augustine feared that he would die before he discovered the truth about this. Still, the faith was daily becoming more a part of his being.

VII:6 Astrology Renounced. Augustine told of his renunciation of astrology during this time, recalling his own obstinate rejection of Nebridius' arguments against astrology as well as those of the wise old man, Vindicianus (see Book IV). Augustine credited God's providence with bringing him Firminus, who related the story of two children, one a slave and one of noble birth, born at the exact-same moment, who had quite predictably opposite histories, despite their exact same horoscope. After hearing this story, Augustine's confidence in astrology completely "dissolved and collapsed."

VII:7 Faith's Struggle. Augustine explained that throughout his search for the origin of evil, he gave assent to God's existence, God's immutability, God's care for His creation, God's salvation

On Astrology

"A true forecast is based not on art but on chance. You, Lord, . . . act on those who consult fortune-tellers and those who are consulted, though they are unaware of it" (VII:6).

Immutability

The idea that God is not susceptible to change.

The Platonic Books

When Augustine spoke of the Platonic books, he was speaking primarily of the writings of Plotinus (c. 205–70), the second-century leader of the Greek school of philosophy called Neoplatonism, and Porphyry (232–304), a disciple of Plotinus whose writings had a significant influence on medieval philosophy. Both philosophers lived and taught in Rome during their mature years.

Transcendence

Above and independent of the material universe, God is transcendent in Being, different from everything in creation, "wholly other." While human beings and the rest of creation are finite and caused by God, He is infinite in character and is uncaused. Humans experience God, but only in so far as God has enabled them to do so—either through their reason or through God's revelation in history.

offered in Christ as revealed in the Scripture. But despite his mental acceptance of these orthodox beliefs, he still found himself struggling and searching.

VII:8 God's Goads. Augustine spoke of the "inward goads" with which God moved Augustine forward until he had reached the point of certainty.

VII:9 Light from the Platonists. Augustine began his discussion of the influence of the "Platonic books" in his journey toward certainty. Augustine made clear that he saw some of the teachings of Scripture anticipated in pagan philosophy. "In them I read, not indeed in these words *but much the same thought, enforced by many varied arguments* [emphasis added], that 'In the beginning was the Word, and the Word was with God, and the Word was God.'" Though grateful for the ways God used these books to shape his faith, the bishop Augustine seemed to have a need to clarify that, though these books were helpful in his faith, they do not contain many things that are central to the Christian gospel.

VII:10 God's Transcendence. Augustine described how he came to understand the transcendence of God, seeing himself "in the region of dissimilarity." Armed with this new understanding, Augustine took a step toward certainty, explaining that once he began to grasp the transcendence of God, "all doubt left" him.

VII:11 The Source of Existence. Augustine concluded that nothing can be said to exist absolutely except God.

VII:12 The Goodness of Existence. Augustine told of his growing recognition, thanks in great measure to his exposure to the Platonic books, that, since evil is the absence of good, everything that exists is good.

VII:13 Evil as Lack. Augustine affirmed that "evil does not exist at all." Describing the world in hierarchical terms, he pictured the creation moving in stages from God, the absolute superior Being, through angels and humans and then to the most inferior things. Augustine told of his growing recognition that evil is, at least in part, a human perception problem. He declared that one should not say, "Would that those things did not exist!" but instead should praise God for them.

VII:14 Light on the Nature of Evil. Augustine gave a brief summary of his search for the origin of evil. Not wanting to attribute any evil thing to God, he came to the conclusion that anything displeasing in creation could not be a part of God's creation, choosing therefore to presume there to be two opposing substances in the world: good and evil. From this foundation, Augustine confessed, he created a god of his own making, "a god pervading all places in infinite space." He told of his coming to understand God's infinity "in another sense" that "did not come from the flesh," a discovery that awakened him in new ways.

Evil—In the Eye of the Beholder

". . . it is no cause for surprise when bread which is pleasant to a healthy palate is misery to an unhealthy one; and to sick eyes light which is desirable to the healthy is hateful" (VII:6).

VII:15 Being—Finite and Infinite. Augustine declared that in God "all things are finite," because they occupy a limited space and because they have a beginning in time, whereas God is beyond time.

VII:16 Levels of Being. Augustine asserted that things that may appear evil (vipers and worms, for example) are actually "well fitted for the lower parts of . . . creation." He reasserted his

"For since the creation of the world God's invisible qualities—his eternal power and divine nature—have been clearly seen, being understood from what has been made, so that men are without excuse" (Rom. 1:20).

Comparing the Impact of the Platonist Books and the Scripture

"It is one thing from a wooded summit to catch a glimpse of the homeland of peace and not to find the way to it. . . . It is another thing to hold on to the way that leads there, defended by the protection of the heavenly emperor" (VII:21).

newfound conclusion that evil is not a substance at all, but simply a lack of being.

VII:17 Shaky Faith. Augustine recalled that he, at this point, already loved God but "did not press on to enjoy my God," identifying his carnal lifestyle as the cause of the weight that held him trapped. With echoes of the Platonic hierarchy, he told of his gradual ascent and his temporary experience of certainty.

"In the flash of a trembling glance" (Chadwick), Augustine declared, he grasped God's "'invisible nature understood through the things which are made' (Rom. 1:20)"; but unable to "keep [the] vision fixed," he "returned to [his] customary condition." He spoke of his intense longing "for what I had, as it were, perceived the aroma of but was not yet able to feed on."

VII:18 Christ—the Mediator. Augustine related his inability to enjoy God, a strength he did not find, until he had embraced Christ the Mediator (1 Tim. 2:5). He admitted that he was held back by his own pride: "To possess my God, the humble Jesus, I was not yet humble enough."

VII:19 Christ—the Word. Augustine described the understanding of Christ to which he had come. Up to this point, Augustine had believed Christ to be only an unparalleled man "of excellent wisdom" but had not yet understood "the mystery of the Word made flesh." His belief in the veracity of Scripture led Augustine to accept that Jesus was fully human, thus avoiding the heretical errors into which Alypius fell for a time.

VII:20 Limitations of Platonism. Augustine described both his growing certainty and his nagging inability to enjoy God, describing himself as "puffed up with knowledge" and prideful. He declared his belief that God designed that he read the "Platonist books" before seriously encountering the Scripture, in order that he might see in stark contrast what essential parts of the gospel were missing in the Platonist books.

VII:21 Light from Scripture. Augustine's understanding became increasingly clear through his personal reading of the Scripture, especially Paul's letters. Augustine found that through face-to-face exposure to Scripture, that which he once thought were contradictions "simply vanished." Augustine repeated that though the Platonist books offered much that was true, they missed much that could only be found in Scripture.

 COMMENTARY

Restlessness. Book VII returns Augustine's readers to the thesis of his entire work and one of the most famous quotes in history: "Our heart is restless until it rests in you." Here Augustine described his restlessness in terms of "inward goads" which made his life "unendurable" until he came to a point of certainty in God. For Augustine, this "unendurable restlessness" is a gift of God, without which he could have easily given up his search and settled into a comfortable agnosticism.

Though the catalyst for Augustine's restlessness, specifically his concerns about substance, mass and the origin of evil, may seem a bit unfamiliar and esoteric to the modern reader, the reality of restlessness certainly is not.

Like Augustine's experience, overwhelming restlessness for moderns is just as likely to come from what might appear to be insignificant causes. Modern restlessness can find its immediate sources in a simple fear of failure, in a lack of consistent distractions, or even in a fear of not being liked. Across the centuries God has used the fragile human tendency toward restlessness as a personal invitation for His children to look beyond themselves. As you reflect on your own pilgrimage, at what times has restlessness characterized that phase of your life? Looking back, can you see a divine purpose in the restlessness?

The Search for the Origin of Evil. When Augustine abandoned his Manichaean beliefs, he also lost a clear solution to the question of the origin of evil. For the Manichaeans, the answer was simple: there was a force apart from God that created evil, a force that God was not strong enough to defeat. As Augustine became clearer in his understanding of the transcendence of God, that God is different from and beyond His creation, he came to acknowledge that all that is not God must, by definition, be part of creation. But this still left Augustine with the fundamental question, If God created everything, does that mean that God created evil? Into this no-man's-land of confusion Augustine was thrown to struggle through his search for the origin of evil.

At this point the books of the Platonists gave Augustine a framework for answering his quite "visceral" (VII:21) search. In the Platonic hierarchy (alluded to in VII:13), everything moves from God (the highest being or the highest good) through successive stages of less and less being, until the created order descends to the level of nonbeing. It is this state of nonbeing, then, that we humans experience as evil. Evil, as Augustine came to learn, is not a substance in and of itself. Evil is the complete absence of being, the complete absence of good.

How did Platonism provide Augustine an understanding of evil that enabled him to move from Manichaeism to Christian faith?

Pride. Augustine used two memorable images to describe how his own pride stood in the way of his embracing Christ, the Mediator. He pictured his own head being so swollen with conceit that it closed his eyes, blinding him to the truth (VII:7). Later in Book VII, he spoke of his inability to "humble himself," to lower himself from his place of pride enough to embrace Christ (VII:18). With fascinating irony, God used

Augustine's quick mind and hunger for learning to draw him to the doorstep of grace, but his pride in that same intellect kept him hesitant to enter in.

BOOK VIII—THE BIRTH PANGS OF CONVERSION

- - - - -

Why People Reject Christ

Augustine admitted that all of his intellectual questions had been answered to his satisfaction yet he remained unable to believe. It was, in fact, not the intellectual questions that had kept him from God but the weight of his own lifestyle, his "habits." In your own life, have intellectual questions blocked the road to faith? Where do you now stand regarding those questions?

"I was an unhappy young man, wretched as at the beginning of my adolescence when I prayed to you for chastity and said: 'Grant me chastity and continence, but not yet. I was afraid you might hear my prayer quickly" (VIII:7).

BOOK-AT-A-GLANCE

1 The Decision to Visit Simplicianus

2–4 The Story of the Conversion of Victorinus

5 The Drowsy Indecision of Habit

6 The Stories of Ponticianus

7–8 The Unhappy Hesitation in the Garden

9–10 The Reflections on the Will

11 The Appearance of Lady Continence

12 The Tears of Conversion

SUMMARY

Book VIII contains the climax of Augustine's conversion story. Through a series of experiences both with friends and in solitude, the chains of Augustine's hesitation were broken, and he chose to embrace the Catholic faith. The book concludes with the story of his conversion in the garden, with his friend, Alypius, watching nearby. He concluded by renouncing his secular ambition and his plans for marriage.

VIII:1 Desire for Stability. After expressing gratitude for God's hand in leading him from instability to certainty, Augustine told of his decision to visit Simplicianus, an older man who was later to succeed Ambrose as bishop of Milan. Augustine told of his struggle between continuing to pursue marriage or choosing a life of celibacy.

VIII:2–3 Victorinus' Conversion. Augustine told of his visit with Simplicianus, the "father to the then bishop Ambrose in the receiving of grace." Simplicianus was delighted by Augustine's exposure to the books of the Platonists, books that were translated into Latin by Victorinus, a Roman Christian. Since Simplicianus was intimately involved in Victorinus' conversion, he related the story to Augustine, introducing Victorinus as a highly esteemed scholar in Rome, who used his quick mind and sharp tongue in the defense of idolatry. Through exposure to the Scripture and "all the Christian books," he eventually came to confess privately to Simplicanus that he was already a Christian. But Simplicanus refused to accept that Victorinus was truly a believer unless he became a part of the church. But fearing offending his non-Christian friends, Victorinus simply laughed and asked, "Then do walls make Christians?" Simplicanus remained resolved in his position, and eventually Victorinus became more concerned about offending Christ than offending public opinion. His baptism and profession of faith came as a shock to the city of Rome and a great encouragement to the church.

Certainty in Uncertainty

"Your words stuck fast in my heart and on all sides I was defended by you. Of your eternal life I was certain, though I saw it 'in an enigma as if in a mirror' . . . . My desire was not to be more certain of you but to be more stable in you. But in my temporal life everything was in a state of uncertainty" (VIII:1).

Today people often say they can be Christians without being church members. How do you evaluate this stance?

Augustine, inspired by the story of Victorinus, pondered why the return of something lost brings more joy than if the thing had never been lost.

VIII:4 Sharing the Joy. Augustine explained that a story like the conversion of Victorinus or the apostle Paul causes "a richer delight" because "many share in the joy," and those who share the story find their excitement "inflamed" by one another.

VIII:5 Chains of Hesitation. Augustine recalled his eagerness to follow the example of Victorinus, who happily gave up "the school of loquacious chattering," when a law was enacted forbidding Christians to teach rhetoric. Augustine recalled that by this time he could no longer use the excuse that he was awaiting certainty about the truth. But still, Augustine said, he felt the chains of hesitation like a drowsiness that overtakes a person who has fully decided to get up but who finds himself saying, "Just a little longer."

VIII:6 The Two Chains. Augustine began the story of his deliverance from the two chains that enslaved him at this time, the chains of "sexual desire" and the "slavery of worldly affairs." After a brief introduction of his close friendship with Alypius, Nebridius, and Verecundus at this time, he told of a surprise visit from Ponticianus, a compatriot from Africa who held a high office in the emperor's court and who was also a baptized believer. He related the well-known story of Antony, the Egyptian monk, a story completely unknown to Augustine and Alypius, who were amazed with the story and surprised to learn of monasteries near Milan. By telling a story of his own, Ponticianus testified of his own firsthand experience with the impact of Antony's story.

"I tell you in the same way there will be more rejoicing in heaven over one sinner who repents than over ninety-nine righteous persons who do not need to repent" (Luke 15:7).

The Enemy's Defeat

"The enemy suffers a severer defeat when he is overcome in a man upon whom he has a greater hold" (VIII:4).

The Drowsiness of Sin

"The burden of the world weighed me down with a sweet drowsiness such as commonly occurs during sleep. The thoughts with which I meditated about you were like the efforts of those who would like to get up but are overcome by deep sleep and sink back again" (VIII:5).

Ponticianus explained that he was walking one day with three other palace officials, a group of four who split into pairs. While he and his companion walked, the other pair arrived at a house where they discovered a book that contained the "Life of Antony." When the two pairs finally reunited at this house, Ponticianus and his partner found the other two "inflamed" by what they had read, resolved to leave their secular vocations and serve God. Ponticianus and his companion returned to their careers, doing so grieving over themselves. Augustine added as a concluding comment that the two who renounced their vocations both had wives who later "dedicated their virginity" to God.

VIII:7 No More Excuses. Augustine revealed how the stories of Ponticianus forced Augustine to pay attention to his own condition. Augustine described how he was torn between feeling great shame in comparison to the young men Ponticianus described and wanting to postpone his decision. He saw himself as one who had made little progress since his adolescent years. Augustine's final excuse, that he had been awaiting certainty about how to direct his course, had now fallen. Though he admitted that "now the day had come in which I was to be laid bare to myself" and that his "insides were being gnawed at and I was greatly perplexed with a horrible shame." Augustine's soul hung back in deathly fear of being delivered from the habit that was leading him to certain death.

VIII:8 The Garden. Augustine vividly described his deep distress (using words like "hot conflict," "healthily deranged," "tossing and turning") just prior to his conversion. An agitated Augustine cried out to Alypius, "What is wrong with us?" and walked into the garden. Alypius followed at a far enough distance not to intrude on his friend's solitude, as Augustine struggled between his desire to commit himself to God and his own will, which was strangely unable to commit.

VIII:9 A Divided Will. Augustine began a reflection on the will, initiated by his recognition of his own inability to commit himself wholeheartedly to God. He asserted that the solution to this apparent division of the will can be found in the fact that though the mind may "rise by truth" it is also "brought down by habit."

VIII:10 Manichaean Error. Augustine continued his reflections on the will with a notable polemic against the beliefs of the Manichaeans, who believe there are two wills, one good and one evil. He argued that there are not two separate wills, "from two contrary principles."

VIII:11 Severe Mercy. Augustine continued his description of his "tossing and turning," vividly portraying God's "severe mercy, redoubling the lashes of fear and shame," which prodded Augustine toward a decision. He personified the "folly of follies" and the "vanity of vanities" as his "old mistresses." They were whispering to him, taunting him . . . asking him if he realized how terrible it would be to be without them forever. On the other side, the chaste lady—Continence—stretched forth to receive him, to embrace him, holding in her holy hands many good examples of chaste men and women who had found joy.

Continence smiled at Augustine, encouraging him to do what all these men and women had done. And yet, they had not done it themselves. God had enabled them to find this joy.

Continence then urged Augustine not to try this himself: "Cast yourself upon Him; fear not, He will not withdraw Himself so that you will fall; cast yourself fearlessly upon Him. He will receive and will heal you."

VIII:12 "Tolle Lege"—"Take and Read." This chapter may easily be considered the climax of *Confessions*, as Augustine here surrenders to God. Augustine recalled being moved to tears through a period of profound self-examination in the garden. He moved further away from Alypius and through his tears heard the chanting of a child, "Pick up and read, pick up and read." He interpreted these words as an explicit command from God (recalling how Antony took the words of a particular Gospel reading as if they were specifically given as an instruction to him). Augustine hurried back to where Alypius was, took up the book, opened it, and read "the first passage on which [his] eyes lit," Romans 13:13–14. By the time he finished reading the passage, he was flooded with relief from anxiety. He related his experience to Alypius, who immediately asked to see the text for himself. Reading the following verse, Romans 14:1, "Receive the person who is weak in faith," Alypius immediately applied the verse to himself; and without hesitation, Alypius joined Augustine in his decision, one which was "entirely congruent" with Alypius' high moral principles and lifestyle. The two immediately related their decision to Monica. She was filled with joy, seeing that God had granted her much more than she had begged for. Augustine explained that the immediate implication of his conversion was that he would no longer seek a wife and would abandon all "ambition for success in this world."

Augustine's Conversion Text

"Let us behave decently, as in the daytime, not in orgies and drunkenness, not in sexual immorality and debauchery, not in dissension and jealousy. Rather, clothe yourselves with the Lord Jesus Christ, and do not think about how to gratify the desires of the sinful nature" (Rom. 13:13–14).

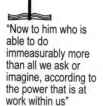

"Now to him who is able to do immeasurably more than all we ask or imagine, according to the power that is at work within us" (Eph. 3:20).

ℵ COMMENTARY

The Process of Conversion. From the very first chapter of Book VIII, the tug-of-war between "the softer option" of marriage and the "narrow paths" of celibacy was at the forefront of Augustine's thinking as he moved through his final steps of conversion. Though it is not until the end of Book VIII that Augustine told of his Damascus-Road-like conversion in the garden, it could easily be argued that Augustine's conversion did not take place suddenly but gradually, making it difficult to pinpoint at exactly what point he passed from death to life. In VII:7, he professed his belief in the essential tenets of a very orthodox faith. In the beginning of Book VIII, he declared that he was at the point of certainty of eternal life, though not stability. He had his conversion experience in the garden at the end of Book VIII, but it was not until his baptism in Book IX that he understood himself to be truly forgiven for his sins.

In what way has your own pilgrimage been similar to Augustine's? In what ways different?

Friendship. In Book VIII, *Confessions* makes clear that the process of conversion, even for the intensely interior Augustine, was not essentially a private matter. Though Augustine spent much time "twisting and turning" alone, it is no surprise that when Augustine was converted, his closest friend was nearby and without hesitation joined Augustine in his conversion.

The symphony of characters involved in Augustine's conversion built to a crescendo through a series of encounters in which he repeatedly identified the traces of God's hand. First, Augustine initiated a visit with Simplicanus, the priest who thirteen years later would succeed Ambrose as bishop, a conversation that essentially grows out of Augustine's disappointment about the unavailability of bishop Ambrose. As it turns out, Simplicianus' familiarity with the very Platonic books that Augustine has been reading is instrumental in Augustine's conversion. Simplicianus' story of the conversion of Victorinus, a story with surprising parallels to Augustine's, even to the point of their common vocation as teachers of rhetoric, sparked Augustine's attention.

If the story of Victorinus sparked his attention, the story of Antony and the conversion of the companions of Ponticianus ignited him and compelled him toward a decision. Again, God used the "frail instrumentality" of Augustine's friends and acquaintances, using "chance" meetings and surprising "coincidences" in the stories told by friends to bring him to the point of surrender in his struggle with God.

Popular Phrases. Book VIII contains two classic phrases that have been picked up and frequently used by other theologians. The phrase "leap of faith," a phrase often associated with the writings of the Danish philosopher, Soren Kierkegaard, may easily have been borrowed from *Confessions* (VIII:11). In recent years, Augustine's phrase "severe mercy" has been frequently attributed to the writings of C. S. Lewis, particularly in a letter which appears in a book by the same title by Sheldon Vanauken.

What's Wrong with Us?

"I turned on Alypius and cried out, 'What is wrong with us? What is this that you have heard? Uneducated people are rising up and capturing heaven, and we with our high culture without any heart. . . . Do we feel no shame at making not even an attempt to follow?'" (VIII:8).

BOOK IX—CASSICIACUM: TO MONICA'S DEATH

"As I read [the Scriptures], I was set on fire, but I did not discover what to do for the deaf and dead of whom I had been one, when I was a plague, a bitter and blind critic barking at the scriptures which drip with the honey of heaven and blaze with your light."

BOOK-AT-A-GLANCE

1–5 Preparing for the New Life

6 Being Baptized with Alypius and Adeodatus

7 Reflecting on Worship and Miracles

8–13 Remembering the Life and Death of Monica

SUMMARY

Book IX recalls the end of Augustine's vocation as a teacher, his time of preparation for baptism at Cassiciacum, his decision to return to Africa, and his remembrance of the life and death of Monica. Augustine recalled her final days in Ostia, a stopping place on their journey to Africa, and spoke of his secret grief over her death. The book tells, as well, of the conversion of his friends Nebridius, Verecundus, and Alypius, as well as that of his son, Adeodatus, who joined Augustine in baptism in Milan.

IX:1 "My Brightness, My Riches, My Health." Augustine spoke with the enthusiasm and freedom of a man who has just been released from bondage.

IX:2 Change of Career. Augustine responded to those who had criticized him for not leaving his teaching vocation immediately after his conversion, choosing instead "quietly to retire from [his] post as a salesman of words." He explained that though he had made the decision not to return to teaching, he continued for about twenty more days until Vintage Vacation, a major break in the school year (from August 22 to October 15). He concluded the chapter nondefensively, admitting that he would not contest those who suggested that he "had sinned in this matter."

IX:3 A Friend's Conversion. Augustine told of the conversion and baptism of Verecundus, whose marriage sadly prevented him from joining Augustine and Alypius on the "journey on which [they] had embarked." Verecundus offered his country estate at Cassiciacum as resting place for Augustine and his companions during their vacation. Augustine also told of the conversion of Nebridius from Manichaean beliefs, reporting that before Nebridius' death, "his whole household had first become Christian." The chapter ends with Augustine's recollection of his continued friendship with Verecundus, whom he exhorted to become faithful in his state as a married man.

IX:4 Time of Assimilation. Augustine recalled memories of God's work during the Vintage Vacation period. As he remembered the struggles of the painful "inward prods" that brought him to God, that memory had now become "sweet." He related how the Psalms aided him in kindling his love for God, how he was "fired by an enthusiasm to recite them," reporting his anger over the error of the Manichees. That anger quickly moved to compassion, as he wished for some way to communicate to them the truth he now knew.

"But sanctify Christ as Lord in your hearts, always being ready to make a defense to everyone who asks you to give an account of the hope that is in you, yet with gentleness and reverence" (1 Peter 3:15, NASB).

He told of a torturous toothache which he understood as "the acute pain of [God's] chastisement," recalling God's merciful healing that took place as soon as he and his companions began to pray. Augustine felt a profound sense of awe at how God worked in this instance. He said he had never seen anything like this.

IX:5 Preparing for Baptism. Augustine told of his resignation from teaching, leaving both because of his new resolve to serve God and because of the physical pain in his chest due to an increased difficulty breathing. He told of a letter of inquiry which he sent to Ambrose, asking him to recommend books of Scripture to read as preparation for baptism. Following the recommendation of Ambrose, Augustine attempted to read the prophet Isaiah but with great difficulty, eventually putting it aside until he had become more accustomed to the style of language used in Scripture.

IX:6 Baptism. Augustine related (in notable brevity) his baptism with his friend Alypius and his son Adeodatus, who was then fifteen. Augustine spoke highly of his son's intelligence and recalled Adeodatus' early death (with sparse detail), grateful that at baptism, they became "the same age . . . in God's grace."

IX:7 The Singing of Hymns. Building on his comments in the previous chapter of the power of church hymns to cause him to weep, Augustine explained the roots of the practice of singing in the church at Milan, a practice that actually grew out of a sharp conflict between the young emperor's Arian mother and Bishop Ambrose. She threatened to take over the churches on Easter of 386, and Ambrose organized a permanent sit-in to prevent the takeover, during

Six Months in Milan Prior to Augustine's Conversion

February—Justina, the Arian mother of the fifteen-year-old emperor, Valentinian II, persecuted followers of bishop Ambrose.
Easter—Ambrose arranged a sit-in to prevent churches being confiscated by military force.
June—The bodies of martyrs, Gervasius and Protasius, were found, stirring up the city.
August—Augustine's conversion took place.

which time hymns were introduced "to prevent the people from succumbing to depression and exhaustion" in the long hours of standing watch. This chapter also tells of Ambrose's discovery of the relics of martyrs, relics that were immediately transferred to Ambrose's basilica, where they had a miraculous effect on many.

IX:8 Evodius. Augustine introduced Evodius, "a young man from [Augustine's] home town" who had joined the group that was now living together in community. The group agreed to move back to Africa together, believing that they could be of the most service to God there.

Evodius joined Augustine in his travels from Milan to Rome and then to Ostia and on to Africa. About 400, Evodius became a bishop and joined Augustine in the conflicts with the Manichees and Pelagians.

Augustine then told of the death of his mother at Ostia, and he spent the remainder of this chapter remembering her story. He told of the "decrepit maidservant" who cared for Monica as a child and attempted to teach her to control her "greedy appetite" for water, knowing that if her thirst was not held to a "respectable moderation," she might easily fall into addiction to wine at a later time. He told of her subsequent obsession with wine and how she was finally rescued through the cutting remark of a slave girl who accused her of being "a boozer."

IX:9 Monica's Faithfulness. Augustine told of his mother's marriage, in which she "served [her husband] as her lord" and patiently endured his unfaithfulness. Her diligent and kind witness eventually lead him to become a baptized believer. Augustine celebrated his mother's servant attitude toward her husband, recalling that

Pelagians

Those who followed the teachings of Pelagius (360–420), a British monk and theologian who held that, like Adam, each human being is created with the power and freedom to choose good or evil. Pelagius argued that each soul is a separate creation of God and hence is not corrupted by Adam's sin. He attributed sin not to corruption of the human will by Adam's sin but to the weakness of human flesh; people inherit not sin but the effects of sin, which impair the flesh. They are free to cooperate with God in the attainment of holiness, using the gifts God gives them—the Bible, reason, and the example set by Jesus Christ. Pelagius's beliefs that God would not necessarily condemn unbaptized infants and that human nature is essentially good brought him into conflict with Augustine.

other wives marvelled at the way Monica dealt with her husband's hot temper. God used Monica's Christian witness in such a way that her husband was converted before his death.

Augustine gives thanks for his mother's gift of being able to reconcile quarreling people, remembering the failure of Monica's maidservants' attempts to stir up a quarrel between her and her mother-in-law, an attempt thwarted by Monica's "persistence in patience and gentleness."

IX:10 Inexhaustible Abundance. Augustine recalled a visionary experience which he and Monica shared together in Ostia before she fell ill. As they talked deeply together, moving higher and deeper in their discussion of spiritual things, they "moved up . . . to the region of inexhaustible abundance." This vision was so compelling for them that from then on, "the world with all its delights" had become "worthless." On this day Monica declared that she did not know what she still had left to do in her life, since her hope in this world had already been fulfilled.

IX:11 Monica's Death. Augustine told of his mother's final days, explaining that within the span of five days of their "vision," his mother became sick, passing in and out of consciousness. With Augustine and his brother at her side, she made requests about her burial, eventually leaving her sons with only one request: "that you remember me at the Lord's altar." Augustine gave thanks that his mother had been freed from anxiety about where she was to be buried.

IX:12 A Son's Grief. Augustine described his private grief over the loss of his mother, keeping himself from weeping, not wanting "to celebrate the funeral with tearful dirges." Augustine described himself as "tortured by a

The Conversion of Patricius

"At the end, when her husband had reached the end of his life in time, she succeeded in gaining him for you. After he was a baptized believer, she had no cause to complain of behavior which she had once tolerated when he was not a believer" (IX:9).

Family Background

Augustine's brother, Navigus, is not mentioned by name in *Confessions*. Most scholars believe that Navigus did not share his brother's religious position, although a number of Augustine's nieces became nuns.

Monica Remembered

". . . she exercised care for everybody as if they were all her children. She served us as if she was a daughter to all of us" (IX:9).

Throughout the *Institutes*, John Calvin relies heavily on the writings of Augustine. But when it comes to Augustine's reflections on praying for Monica after her death, Calvin says this was a case in which Augustine didn't test his practice by the norm of Scripture.

twofold sadness," first over the loss of his mother and then over the power that grief held over him. Though surrounded by many friends, Augustine hid his sadness from them to the extent that they "supposed [him] to have no feeling of grief." Later, after a time of rest, he found that much of his suffering had been relieved. And at this point, he wept for his mother.

IX:13 Requiem. Augustine prayed for his mother, asking God to forgive her sins, confident that God had already answered this prayer, and he invited all his readers to remember both of his parents at God's altar.

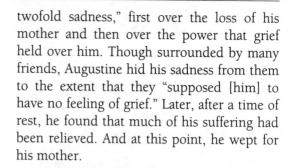

COMMENTARY

The End of the Story. With Book IX, Augustine's linear autobiography comes to an end. It seems obvious that his intent in the first nine chapters was simply to tell the story of his conversion, not to tell the story of his life. It is a fascinating coincidence that Augustine's life of ministry began as his mother's life came to an end. Perhaps he concluded his autobiography with the death of his mother to convey vividly that the baton of faith had been passed from his mother to him, and his own life of faith after conversion was another story.

Though it would have been natural for him to do otherwise, Augustine included only sketchy autobiographical information about his life as a bishop or even the intense controversies he faced against the Manichees, the Pelagians, and the Donatists. Whether he ever imagined that his story would have a much wider impact than even the popularity of Antony's conversion is doubtful. But the fact that his story (primarily that found in these nine chapters) has continued to leave its mark on generations for almost sixteen centuries indicates that much of his story is universal to the Christian experience across cultures and the centuries.

Longing. Part of the timeless appeal of *Confessions* is the way he portrayed with such clarity the sheer delight, the glimpse of heaven, that seems to be granted to believers in every time and place. But Augustine's descriptions clearly declare that such experiences are temporary and that, for the most part, the Christian life on this side of heaven includes a longing for what can only be held in heaven.

In Book IX, Augustine repeatedly alluded to the longing for God that is inherent in any vital spiritual life. He spoke passionately of this longing, in his description of the death of his friend, Nebridius, describing his transformed life in the presence of God.

Even more vivid is his description of the fierce longing for God experienced in the vision at Ostia with his mother, telling of his tasting of the presence of God in such a profound way that all human pleasures pale in comparison.

Trouble Understanding the Scripture. It is fascinating that a man as brilliant as Augustine had such difficulty with the language of Scripture, even after his conversion. Much of his difficulty may be attributed to the fact that only a poor translation was available, but it is worthy of note that this great man of faith was initially unable to complete his first Scripture reading assignment.

From the way allusions to Scripture weave in and out of almost every chapter of *Confessions*, it

Experiencing God

As he ended the story of his conversion, Augustine's writing drove a stake in the ground of his memory, confirming and retelling his experience both from an external (what he and Monica talked about) and an internal (the intensity of the longing for God which he felt) perspective. Is it the (re)birthright of every believer to have at least one vivid experience of the presence of God, or do some people of strong faith never have an experience like this?

Nebridius in Heaven

"He no longer pricks up his ear when I speak, but puts his spiritual mouth to your fountain and avidly drinks as much as he can of wisdom, happy without end. I do not think him so intoxicated by that as to forget me, since you, Lord, whom he drinks, are mindful of us" (IX:3).

Great Longing

"If only it could last. . . . Then this alone could ravish and absorb and enfold in inward joys the person granted the vision. So too eternal life is of the quality of that moment of understanding after which we sighed" (IX:10).

is clear that Augustine eventually overcame his lack of understanding. It may be normative for new Christians to have difficulty feeling at home with the Scriptures, but Augustine's story certainly proves that a new believer's hesitancy to study the Scripture need not be permanent.

Details. Although Augustine gave such sparse detail about his baptism (much less, in fact, than he gave about the baptism of Victorinus), he went into a much more extensive description of the seemingly less significant topic of the origins of hymn singing in Milan.

Grief. Augustine's hidden grief over his mother may appear oddly suppressed to the modern reader. He contrasts his controlled approach to that of his son, Adeodatus, who cried out without inhibition. Augustine wanted to cry out but reserved this only for God's ears. He expressed displeasure over the fact that these kinds of emotions were a part of the human condition.

BOOK X—MEMORY

What difficulties did Augustine have with Scripture? In what ways does your own relationship to Scripture parallel Augustine's? In what ways does it differ from his? What did Augustine do regarding his difficulty in reading and understanding Scripture?

"Why then should I be concerned for human readers to hear my confessions? It is not they who are going to 'heal my sicknesses' (Ps. 102:3). The human race is inquisitive about other people's lives, but negligent to correct their own. Why do they demand to hear from me what I am when they refuse to hear from you what they are?" (X:3).

BOOK-AT-A-GLANCE

1–5 The Shift from "Who I Once Was" to "Who I Am"

6–7 The Ascent from the External to the Internal

8–19 The Mystery of Memory

20–23 The Quest for the Happy Life

24–27 The Search for God

28–40 The Examination of Conscience

41–43 Christ the True Mediator

SUMMARY

In Book X, the focus of *Confessions* shifts from the past to the present tense. After giving his extensive reflections on the role of memory in the search for God, Augustine examined his own conscience before God, seeking God's guidance to show him the places where he had fallen into sin.

X:1–5 Reasons for Confession. Augustine seemed particularly aware of his readers, as he prayed for their edification, acknowledging that he was only confessing what God already knew.

Responding to the apparent questions of those who have been curious about Augustine's current condition, he leaped forward ten years in his story to speak in the present tense, acknowledging not what he was but what he now is. He confesses his utter dependence on God to give the light to allow him to understand clearly who he has become.

X:6–7 What Is This Love? Augustine told of his experience of God through five spiritual senses. He confirmed his intention to rise above the mere physical capacities that he shared with "the horse and mule," declaring that the experience of the love of God will not come through the senses of the body.

X:8–12 Marvelous Capacities. Augustine described his "rising by degrees to him who

"If he finds fault that I wept for my mother for a fraction of an hour, . . . let him not mock me but rather, . . . let him weep himself before [God] for my sins" (IX:12).

Hiding from God

"What could be hidden within me, even if I were unwilling to confess it to you? I would be hiding you from myself, not myself from you" (X:2).

What Do I Love?

"——a light, voice, odor, food, embrace of my inner man, where my soul is floodlit by light which space cannot contain, where there is sound that time cannot seize, where there is a perfume which no breeze disperses, where there is a taste for food no amount of eating can lessen, and where there is a bond of union that no satiety can part. That is what I love when I love my God" (X:6).

"This power of memory is great, very great, my God. It is a vast and infinite profundity. Who has plumbed its bottom? This power is that of my mind and is a natural endowment, but I myself cannot grasp the totality of what I am" (X:8).

How Do We Learn?

Augustine echoed the principle of memory contained in Socrates' dialogue with Meno, in which an uneducated slave is able to declare a complex mathematical principle simply through responding to questions. The conclusion of the dialogue is that learning is essentially remembering, making conscious what was already present in the memory.

made me." His journey takes him through the "fields and spacious palaces" of memory. Augustine paused here to express wonder at the capacity of memory and all that is contained there. Sometimes we bring forth a memory instantly. Sometimes it takes a little longer. Other times, memories come rushing at us like troops—unbidden. And we want to send them away. Some come in fragments. Others in "unbroken order."

He questioned where the capacity to understand and categorize comes from if not through images. Answering his own question, he declared, "The answer must be that they were already in the memory" (X:10). Augustine went on to express his amazement in the memory's ability to categorize concepts (X:11) and grasp numbers and mathematical concepts (X:12).

X:13–16 Mind and Memory. Augustine reflected further on the mystery of the memory, marveling at its paradoxes: Mistaken ideas can be remembered correctly (X:13). Negative emotions can be remembered happily (for example, "I happily remember a physical pain that has passed away") (X:14). Physical health can be remembered even in sickness (X:15). And forgetfulness itself can be remembered (X:16). He referred to the memory as "the stomach of the mind" where "gladness and sadness . . . can there be stored; but they cannot be tasted" (X:14).

X:17 From Memory to God. Augustine continues to express wonder at the human capacity for memory. He notes that this is an ability that we share to some extent with beasts and birds. How else could they so precisely find their homes. As marvelous as memory is, Augustine wants to move beyond it. He wants to "arrive at him who hath separated me from the four-footed beasts and made me wiser than the fowls of the air, I will pass beyond memory also, and where shall I find you, Thou truly good and certain sweetness?"

X:18–19 The Joy of Finding. Augustine considered the search for lost things, first recalling the biblical story of the woman and her lost coin (X:18) and then considering the memory's search for recalling something it has lost (X:19).

X:20–23 Thirst for Happiness. Augustine identified God with happiness ("When I seek for you, my God, my quest is for the happy life"), concluding that since the desire for happiness is universal, that desire must have been "held in the memory" (X:20). He declared that happiness lies in God alone and that true happiness is always based in truth, explaining that a person's love for an object can become a substitute for the love of the truth.

X:24–27 God's Gracious Initiative. Augustine sought to understand in which part of his consciousness God could be found, searching in various parts of his memory and finally confessing, "You were not there." And yet Augustine admitted to God paradoxically that God had "deigned to dwell in my memory since the time I learnt about you" (X:25, Chadwick). He went on to question how the immutable God could ever be known, affirming that such knowledge comes only from God's initiative.

X:28–29 Grace in Temptation. Augustine introduced his reflections on temptation, acknowledging his struggle and praying for grace to be obedient, using the prayer that would become a

"As I rise above memory, where am I to find you? My true good and gentle source of reassurance, where shall I find you? If I find you outside my memory, I am not mindful of you. And how shall I find you if I am not mindful of you?" (X:17).

Christian Happiness

"There is a delight which is given not to the wicked, but to those who worship you for no reward save the joy that you yourself are to them. This is the authentic happy life, to set one's joy on you, grounded in you and caused by you. That is the real thing, and there is no other" (X:22).

recurring refrain, "give what you command, and command what you will."

X:30 Lascivious Impulses. Augustine confessed that although he had refrained from sexual activity, the thoughts of his past exploits continued to haunt him, particularly in his sleep. He prayed for God to heal the diseases of his soul as they continued to show up in his dreams.

X:31 Gluttony. Seeking a balance between eating for the sake of health and eating for the sake of "dangerous pleasure," Augustine confessed his battle against gluttony, acknowledging that in this area he sought a middle course "between laxity and austerity." With multiple biblical allusions, he indirectly addressed the Manichaean fascination with pure and impure foods, declaring that it is not the impurity of food he fears but, rather, uncontrolled desire.

X:32 Perfumes. Though Augustine declared that the "allurement of perfumes is not a matter of great concern" to him, he hastened to acknowledge the possibility of blindness to his own vulnerabilities.

X:33 Seeking Balance. Augustine described his temptations to sin with his hearing, confessing that music itself moved him rather than the text being sung. He sees this as a sin but, with typical self-questioning, he admitted that he sometimes erred in being too hard on himself.

X:34 The Good and the Best. Though he acknowledged that God made His creation very good, Augustine was concerned that he not become distracted by created things and forget that it is God who is good. He recognized that humans have made many things that go "far beyond nec-

God's Initiative in the Five Spiritual Senses

"Late have I loved you, beauty so old and so new: late have I loved you. And see, you were within and I was in the external world and sought you there, and in my unlovely state I plunged into those lovely created things which you made. You were with me, and I was not with you. The lovely things kept me far from you, though if they did not have their existence in you, they had no existence at all. You called and cried out loud and shattered my deafness. You were radiant and resplendent, you put to flight my blindness. You were fragrant, and I drew in my breath and now pant after you. I tasted you, and I feel but hunger and thirst for you. You touched me, and I am set on fire to attain the peace which is yours" (X:27).

essary and moderate requirements" and have the power to "entrap the eyes" of men.

X:35 Empty Distractions. Augustine addressed the temptation of "a certain vain and curious desire, veiled under the title of knowledge and learning." Whether watching "mangled carcases," spectacles in theatres, "searching out the hidden powers of nature," or demanding "signs and wonders" from God, not for a purpose that will honor God but just for the thrill of it, Augustine acknowledged the dangers of empty distractions.

X:36–39 Pride's Subtleties. Augustine thanked God for what He had begun to do in taking away Augustine's desire to be vindicated. He acknowledged that he still desired the praise of people and that he relished being feared or loved. He recognized that this tendency stands in the way of his delighting in the truth of God. (X:36). Augustine grieved over the fact that he is more moved when he is praised or when he is blamed unjustly than when one of his fellowmen is praised or criticized unjustly. He prayed that the Lord will put "this madness far from me" (X:37). Augustine confessed the subtlety of pride. He felt contempt for the love of human praise and recognized that this contempt can be a source of pride and sense of superiority! (X:38). While the desire to be praised is a snare, the attitude which says, "I don't care what others think of me," is equally dangerous (X:39).

X:40 Occasional Rest. Recalling the theme of the soul's finding its rest in God, Augustine tells God that only in Him can he find safety from all of these temptations that constantly parade before his mind and from the habits that are still in place and which pull him down. Nevertheless

The Extravagance of Creation

Since God's creation itself goes way beyond "moderate requirements" and pragmatic purposes, how can Christians enjoy the extravagance of God's creation without becoming entangled and distracted from God?

"You see how my heart trembles and strains in the midst of all these perils and others of a like kind. It is not as though I do not suffer wounds, but I feel rather that you heal them over and over again" (X:39, Pine-Coffin).

What has been the impact on your own life and relationship with God in witnessing the early stages of Augustine's journey?

Augustine has a strong sense that all of the components of who he is are contained in God, although as yet he doesn't see how they fit together. At times his sense of God's guidance and God's knowledge of him is incredibly sweet. On these occasions, Augustine has intimations of a perfection that is realized only beyond this world.

X:41–43 True Mediator. Augustine declared the need for a mediator between sinful humans and a perfect God. He concluded with an ascription of praise for Christ, the true Mediator.

COMMENTARY

As Bishop Augustine began Book X, it is obvious that his focus had changed. His muted concern for his listeners in the first nine books became extremely obvious as he related his concern for readers, likely thinking primarily of the flock under his care as bishop of Hippo. He prayed that their hearts would be stirred up by his confessions of his past sins, giving special attention toward those who might be in danger of falling into the sleep of despair over their own sins (X:3). His implicit desire seemed to be that God would use his book to awaken his readers, challenging those who may have read his story out of idle speculation to examine their own lives.

"I myself cannot grasp the totality of what I am" (X:8), and later, "I find my own self hard to grasp" (X:16). In this context his reflections on both memory and temptations can best be understood.

The Shift in Spiritual Disciplines. From the vantage point of his current life as a bishop, Augustine now reflected back on his first nine books, as if it were an entirely different exercise from the one he began in this book. As Augustine moved from Book IX to Book X, he made a fundamental shift in focus. He moved from the spiritual discipline of spiritual autobiography to the spiritual discipline of the examination of conscience.

It makes sense, therefore, that Book X contains much of Augustine's search to understand himself, a search which led Augustine to confess repeatedly the limitations of his own self-understanding.

Augustine's approach to his own self-examination can be instructive for moderns who seek to experience the clarity and depth that the spiritual discipline of examining the conscience can bring. Augustine did not simply reflect in general about his temptations and sins but used the clear structure of the five senses as a springboard, a guide to his reflections, confessing the sins of his sight, his hearing, his tasting, his feeling, and even his smelling.

Obedience. Throughout the final third of Book X, Augustine returned to a familiar refrain, "Grant what you command, and command what you will" (X:28), modeling for his readers an intentional surrender to God's authority and a purposeful dependence on God's power to work in him. For Augustine, obedience is not about a cold sense of duty and drudgery. Instead, he equated obedience to God with supreme happiness, as throughout *Confessions* he described the sheer pleasure and sweet delight of experiencing God—a pleasure which he had tasted enough of to sigh and yearn for an eternity of such joy.

Friendship. As Augustine moved from considering his past to considering his present condition, there is a notable dearth of references on the influence of friendship. Instead, Augustine offered his confession of his own need to be

Spiritual Disciplines

In recent years, there has been an increased fascination with the Christian discipline of journaling. What would be the impact on the church if this trend were taken a step further, with believers giving focus to their journaling by using the spiritual disciplines of autobiography and examination of conscience?

Hearing God's Counsel

"You reply clearly, but not all hear you clearly. All ask your counsel on what they desire, but do not always hear what they would wish. Your best servant is the person who does not attend so much to hearing what he himself wants as to willing what he has heard from you" (X:26).

feared and loved by people. With a distinctive echo of his concerns about the dangers of friendship (described early in *Confessions*), he acknowledged that the person who longs for human praise when God is not pleased with him, is in a vulnerable position even though he is surrounded by human support (X:36). And in the final chapter, Augustine gave his readers a hint of his never fulfilled desire to live a solitary life as a hermit: "Terrified by my sins and the dead weight of my misery, I had turned my problems over in my mind and was half determined to seek refuge in the desert. But you forbade me to do this and gave me strength" (X:43, Pine-Coffin).

"Lord, I cast all my troubles on you and from now on *I shall contemplate the wonders of your law.* You know how weak I am and how inadequate is my frailty. Your only Son, *in whom the whole treasury of wisdom and knowledge is stored up,* has redeemed me with his blood. *Save me from the scorn of my enemies,* for the price of my redemption is always in my thoughts. I eat it and drink it and minister it to other; and as one of the poor I long to be filled with it, to be one of those who *eat and have their fill*" (X:43, Pine-Coffin).

BOOK XI—TIME AND ETERNITY

"All these praise you, the creator of everything. But how do you make them? The way, God, in which you made heaven and earth was not that you made them either in heaven or earth. Nor was it in air or in water, for these belong to heaven and earth. Nor did you make the universe within the framework of the universe. There was nowhere for it to be made before it was brought into existence. Nor did you have any tool in your hand to make heaven and earth. How could you obtain anything you had not made as a tool for making something? What is it for something to be unless it is because you are? Therefore you spoke and they were made, and by your word you made them" (XI:5).

BOOK-AT-A-GLANCE

1 Augustine's Purpose

2–3 Prayer for Illumination

4–5 Reflections on the Beginning of Creation

6–9 Eternal Word

10–14 Reply to Error

15–22 Existence of Past and Future

23–30 Search for an Understanding of Time

31 Ascription of Praise

SUMMARY

This book contains Augustine's reflections on time and eternity, at least in part answering the skeptic's question, "What was God doing before He created the world?" Augustine affirms that God is outside of time, since time itself is a part of His created order.

Spiritual Time Line

When is the last time you recalled your spiritual life story, either in solitude or with others who could be "stirred up" in their love for God?

XI:1 Augustine's Purpose. Augustine gave the rationale for writing his ordered account of so many things, explaining that his goal was to stir up love for God in himself and in his readers.

XI:2–3 Prayer for Illumination. After an extremely brief explanation of why he chose not to tell the story of his call to ministry and God's work in his life as a priest, Augustine asked God to reveal the meaning of the pages of the Scripture, intent to search for the treasures of God, beginning with Genesis 1.

XI:4–5 What Creation Declares. Augustine affirmed that the creation itself declares that it was made because it suffers change and variation, acknowledging that in comparison to God heaven and earth are deficient in beauty and goodness and being. He argued that when God created the world He did not do so as a human craftsman might build something, because it was made without the aid of any tool except God's own word.

XI:6–9 God's Word and Human Words. Augustine compared the human word (which sounds and then passes away) with God's eternal Word, clarifying that God did not create the world with a transient word. Instead, he asserted, when God created the world, He spoke by the Word that was always with God (XI:7). He explained that the eternal reason determines when everything begins and ceases. (XI:8). He confessed that this eternal Word is the unchanging constant, the "fixed point" to which God's people can return, concluding this section by speaking personally about the impact of the eternal Word in his own life.

XI:10–14 A Misunderstanding. Augustine replied to those who ask, "What was God doing before He made heaven and earth?" answering that those who ask such questions have a fundamental misunderstanding of the nature of God and of eternity. (XI:11). Rejecting a tempting flippant reply, he gave a clear, concise response of his own: When we think about what God was doing before He created anything, we necessarily frame this in terms of time—the succession of one event after another. To those who stand amazed that God would wait countless ages before creating the world, Augustine corrected by saying, "Time could not elapse before you made time. . . . There was no 'then' when there was no time," affirming that for God, all "years" exist "in simultaneity" (XI:13), not passing one after the other.

XI:15–19 Duration. Augustine considered inaccuracy inherent in the terms "a long time" and "a short time." For duration to be long or short,

Getting Personal

"What is the light which shines right through me and strikes my heart without hurting? It fills me with terror and burning love: with terror inasmuch as I am utterly other than it, with burning love in that I am akin to it. Wisdom, wisdom it is which shines right through me, cutting a path through the cloudiness" (XI:9).

No Time

"There was therefore no time when you had not made something, because you made time itself" (XI:14).

it has to exist. But it doesn't exist. Past is no longer and future is not yet. He admitted his own lack of clarity on this point when he said that he was investigating such questions and not making assertions. Continuing his investigation, he proposed that future and past events can only exist in the present, either in recollection (past) or in expectation (future) (XI:18). He went on to ask how God informs souls of future events but eventually confessed his own inability to comprehend such concepts.

XI:20–22 Speaking of Time. Beginning with the assumption that neither future nor past exists, Augustine proposed a more accurate vocabulary for speaking of time: (1) "the present considering the past" or "memory," (2) "the present considering the present" or "immediate awareness," and (3) "the present considering the future" or "expectation." He argued that though the common usage of the words "past," "present," and "future" are literally incorrect, they can still be useful even as "inexact" language.

Augustine attempted to determine exactly what is measured when people say they are measuring time (XI:21), concluding that it is neither the present (because it has no extension) nor the past or future (because something that does not exist cannot be measured).

Augustine appealed for God's help in solving this intricate enigma, confessing his incompetence to do so. Though obviously aware that discussions of time are commonplace and easily understood, he holds firmly to his assertion that both what time is and how it is measured remain obscure.

XI:23–25 What Time Is Not. Augustine refuted the learned proposition that the motion of the heavenly bodies constitutes time (XI:23), arguing that even if all the heavenly bodies were no longer present, a spinning potter's wheel would be enough to allow for the marking of time (XI:25). Confessing his own ignorance in understanding time, Augustine spoke with obvious irony as he wrote of "the long period" he had already spent speaking of time (XI:25). Questioning how he knows this while not knowing what time is, Augustine answers by saying that he may know what time is but simply may not be able to articulate it.

XI:26–27 Measuring Time. Augustine considered how it was that he could measure time when he did not know what he was measuring. He suggested (and quickly rejected) the explanation that time can be measured in recitation by the number of lines, feet, and syllables in a poem (XI:26). He presented the example of two sounding voices, one which begins and ends and one which begins but has no end, declaring that the first can be measured (because it has a beginning and an ending) but the second cannot. He gave the additional example of measuring time through the recitation of an eight-syllable phrase, in which it was obvious that the long syllables were twice as long as the short. He concluded that it was not the syllables that he was measuring but, rather, something in his memory that remains fixed in his mind. He asserted that it was not the stream of past events that was being measured but present consciousness.

XI:28 Succession. Augustine illustrated the distinction between present consciousness and past events with the experience of reciting a Psalm, which proceeds from expectation of what is about to be said (future), through the individual syllables (present), and finally into the memory of what has been spoken (past). Augustine concluded that the same principle of the linear successiveness of time holds true for the process of understanding the life span of any individual or even the total history of humankind.

XI:29–30 Two Principles. Augustine then applied his understanding of time to his own desire to leave behind former days and his longing to move toward those things which are unchanging. He told of his yearning for the day when he would find stability in God and summarized his two foundational principles about time: (1) Before time itself began, God existed in eternity. (2) There are no created things, including time, which are "coeternal" with God.

XI:31 God's Perspective. Augustine used his reflections on time as a springboard for acknowledging the depth of the mystery of God. He contrasted the greatest human knowledge with God's eternal knowledge that sees everything not in linear fashion but through the unchangeable eyes of eternity.

Faith and Reason

Augustine, without apology, included the language of faith in his philosophical reflections. What effect would it have on contemporary scientific, political, or philosophical discussions if one or more parties made their case not only from the best resources of reason available but also from the posture of prayer, bound by a certainty of God's transcendent wisdom?

COMMENTARY

From Personal to Philosophical. The pages of Book XI in some ways read more like a philosophical treatise than a personal confession to God. But Augustine's method was radically different than that of most (if not every) traditional work of philosophy in that he rooted his philosophical reflections in the context of prayer.

Science and Faith. While many today might be comfortable with the opposition of piety and reason, Augustine chose to hold these together as complementary components in the search for truth. He refused to place his love for God in a comfortable, private religious category, admitting no contradiction between his intense piety and his earnest scientific or philosophical investigation.

Before Creation. Augustine's response to those who asked what God was doing before He created the world provides both a sensitive and a conclusive answer to any who raise questions that begin "Why did God . . . ?" After rejecting the shallowness of a flippant response to a serious question about God, Augustine simply affirmed that God acts for God's own reasons, reasons to which humans are not often privy. He left the full understanding of the reasons for God's actions in the unsearchable mind of God alone.

Philosophy and Worship. For Augustine, to understand time is to understand God more fully, a basic assumption he made clear in the first chapter of Book XI. Admittedly, Augustine could not help but allow his theology to inform his conclusions; but more strikingly, he allowed the results of his philosophical conclusions to stir him to love God more, to see more clearly God's "profound mystery" (XI:31). His reflections on time climaxed as he expressed his own eager longing for that day when he would share in God's eternity.

The Unacceptable Flippant Reply

"What was God doing before he made heaven and earth? . . .He was preparing hells for people who pry into mysteries" (XI:12, Pine-Coffin).

BOOK XII—PLATONIC AND CHRISTIAN CREATION

"In my needy life, Lord, my heart is much exercised under the impact made by the words of your holy

scripture. All too frequently the poverty of human intelligence has plenty to say, for inquiry employs more words than the discovery of the solution; it takes longer to state a request than to have it granted, and the hand which knocks has more work to do than the hand which receives. We hold on to the promise, which none can make null and void" (XII:1).

BOOK-AT-A-GLANCE

1 The Search to Understand Scripture

2–13 Creation Out of Formlessness

14–16 Comments to Critics

17–22 Variant Interpretations of Scripture

23–27 The Intent of the Author Versus the Truth Conveyed in the Text

28–31 Variety of Edifying Truths

32 The Search for God's Truth in the Intention of the Author

SUMMARY

Book XII contains Augustine's reflections on the first few words of Genesis, his response to critics who disagree with his interpretations, and his guidance for weighing a variety of possible true interpretations. Though not obvious to modern readers, this book also represents Augustine's attempt at reconciling Christian and Platonic views of creation.

XII:1 Trustworthy Promises. Augustine confessed that the words of Scripture had stirred him to search, admitting that those who are searching often use more words than those who have found the solution.

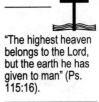

"The highest heaven belongs to the Lord, but the earth he has given to man" (Ps. 115:16).

XII:2 Heaven and Earth. Augustine began his twofold interpretation of the creation of heaven and earth: (1) "Heaven" refers to the "heaven of heaven" which is unseen. (2) "Earth" refers to the visible heaven (sky and stars) and earth.

XII:3–4 Creation of Earth. Augustine explained more about the creation of the earth described in Genesis 1:2, explaining that this earth, "invisible and without form," was, at this time, simply made up of matter which had "no colour, no shape, no body, no spirit" (XII:3). He explained that the words "earth" and "deep" or "abyss" were used in Scripture to help convey this truth to those of duller minds (XII:4), since the concept of formless matter is difficult to understand.

XII:5–6 Matter Without Form. Admitting the difficulty of understanding how matter could be formless, Augustine praised God for "all that [God] disentangled for [him] in examining this question." He went on to describe formless matter as "a nothing something" or "a being which is non-being" (XII:6).

XII:7 Hierarchy of Creation. Augustine explained the hierarchy of creation in Platonic terms: Those beings closer to God are more like Him. Those farther from Him are less like Him. Augustine asserted that God did not create heaven and earth out of Himself or His own substance but created them out of nothing. He argued that if God had created the world out of Himself, creation would be equal to the Creator.

XII:8 Stages of Creation. Augustine clarified that when God first made the earth it was not like the earth his readers might picture, "for it was 'invisible and without form.'" He implied that it might be more accurate to say that God made this almost nothing out of nothing and that out of this almost nothing, God made the visible world. Augustine distinguished between the firmament in the sky, which was on the second day called "heaven," and the "heaven of this heaven." He explained that because this creation came from the "invisible and unorganized earth . . . from this next-to-nothing," it was "mutable," subject to change and decay.

XII:9 Genesis 1:1–2. Augustine reasoned that Moses was silent about days and times in the first two verses of Genesis because when God created the formlessness, there was no time. He explained that the "heaven of heaven," though not coeternal with God, still somehow participates in God's eternity because it cleaves so closely to God that it doesn't change in the way that other parts of creation change.

XII:10 Thirst for Understanding. Augustine returned to God, "panting after God's fountain," asking God to instruct him in the mysteries of the Scriptures.

XII:11 In Summary. Augustine summarized and enhanced much of what he had written in the previous chapters of Book XII: (1) that God is eternal and His will does not change; (2) that the only thing God did not create is "what has no existence"; (3) that any movement away from God is a move toward less being and that such movement is sin; (4) that even the "heaven of heaven," which does not change, is not coeternal with God; (5) that God is "far above time . . . in [his] eternity," and that the soul's "thirsting" for God is a longing for this "heaven of heaven"; (6) that "there is an inexpressible formlessness in the changes undergone by the lowest

> "In the beginning God created the heavens and the earth. And the earth was formless and void, and darkness was over the surface of the deep; and the Spirit of God was moving over the surface of the waters. Then God said, 'Let there be light'; and there was light" (Gen. 1:1–3, NASB).

The Platonic Connection

Augustine's understanding of the creation of the "heaven of heaven" is similar to the concept of the "world-soul" described by Porphyry (the Neoplatonist). The world-soul is a part of the created order that eternally contemplates the divine.

and most inferior creatures"; and (7) that this formlessness is outside of the realm of time.

XII:12 Heaven of Heaven. Augustine affirmed that two things in God's creation are outside of time but still not coeternal with God: the "heaven of heaven" and the "formlessness." Both of these things were made "in the Beginning" before there were days. Formlessness is not "nothing" although it is invisible.

XII:13 Provisional Understanding. Augustine confessed that his interpretation was only his "provisional understanding," his "interim judgement," explaining again that Genesis 1:1–2 describes the creation of two things that are outside of time.

XII:14 Levels of Interpretation. Augustine contemplated the simplicity and the profundity of Scripture. The simplicity attracts us to Scripture. But as we work with Scripture we realize its depths and we are both awed and thrilled. Like the psalmist praying that God would slay the wicked, Augustine prays that God would slay the enemies of Scripture. Having died to themselves, he prays further that God would make these enemies alive to Him. He admitted that others have a different interpretation of Genesis and comes before God laying out these differences, recognizing that he and those with whom he differs belong to God who knows all.

XII:15 An Aside to Opponents. Stepping periodically out of his characteristic conversation with God to address his opponents directly, Augustine replied to those with a different interpretation. He appealed to the inner authority for his interpretation and reiterated (a bit more combatively) many of his previous arguments.

XII:16 Response to Critics. Augustine responded to two types of critics. He showed little patience for the first group, those who denied that his interpretation was true, and appealed to God to be the arbiter between the second group (who did not deny the essential truths of Augustine's interpretation but on some point contradicted it) and himself.

XII:17–21 Four Interpretations. Augustine described four different interpretations of the meaning of the phrase, "heaven and earth" in Genesis 1:1 (XII:17). After declaring that he did not wish to "quarrel about words," he suggested that it was possible to discover a true exegesis of a text, even if that exegesis was not what the author originally had in mind (XII:18). He then listed a set of ten propositions which represent a basic summary of those beliefs that Augustine believed to be foundational to any accurate interpretation of the first chapter of Genesis (XII:19), declaring that these propositions are true and not doubted by those whom God has enabled to see with an inward eye (XII:20). On the basis of these propositions, he presented five possible views of how God created heaven and earth (XII:20) and then gave five possible interpretations of Genesis 1:2.

XII:22 God Alone Is Eternal. Augustine specifically sought to give an answer to those who have difficulty believing anything that is not explicit in the Scripture, in particular that God created the world out of formlessness. He argued that even though the Scripture does not explicitly mention "the creation of the Cherubim and Seraphim" or the creation of other powers described by Paul, orthodox believers have no doubt that God made them all.

XII:23 Interpreting Scripture. Augustine explains that "two areas of disagreement can arise" in matters of interpretation. The first is the truth of the interpretation in question; the second is the original intent of the author. Augustine declares that he will have nothing to do "with those who think they know things but are actually wrong" (e.g., Augustine's conversation of Faustus, the Manichee "expert") or with those who would suggest that "Moses could have said anything untrue." He declares his intent to associate with those who desire to discern God's will "through the intention of [God's] servant" Moses.

XII:24 Interpretive Humility. Augustine urged his readers to modesty in interpretation, affirming that although all number of propositions may be true and consistent with a text, determining exactly which meaning the author had in mind when he wrote those texts is more difficult, if not impossible.

XII:25 Response to Critics. Augustine attacked his critics who arrogantly asserted that they knew what Moses meant and others didn't know what he meant. He pointed out that confidently believing some proposition doesn't make it true. He rejected the idea that truth can be a matter of private interpretation.

XII:26–27 Moses' Intent. Augustine asserted that if he had been in Moses' position he would have desired to write words that could be comprehended both by those who are childlike and those who are sophisticated.

XII:28 Creation: Key Truths. Before relating a variety of interpretations of God's creation, Augustine reviewed some foundational propositions in understanding God's creation: (1) that God transcends all time, while at the same time,

Interpretive Humility

"Which of us . . . can confidently say 'This is what Moses meant . . .' as confidently as he can say, 'Whether Moses meant this or something else, this is true'" (XII:24).

No Private Interpretation

"We must dread your judgements, O Lord, because your truth is not mine alone nor does it belong to this man or that. It belongs to us all, because we all hear your call to share it and you give us dire warning not to think it ours alone, for fear that we may be deprived of it" (XII:25, Pine-Coffin).

making everything in the "time-conditioned creation," (2) that God created the world out of nothing, not out of anything in Himself, and (3) that in God's good creation, there exists a "graded hierarchy of being," from those things closest to God to those furthest away.

XII:29 Analogies for Understanding Creation. Augustine discussed four "priorities" that can be used to help an interpreter understand the creation: "priority in eternity" (i.e., God is prior to everything), "priority in time" (i.e., the blossom is prior to the fruit), "priority in preference" (i.e., the fruit is to be preferred over the blossom), and "priority in origin" (the sound is prior to the song). He explained that in the same way that sound is prior to song but occurs at the same instant, so the created order began with formlessness (sound) and was at the same instant given form (the song).

XII:30–31 God's Way with Scripture. Augustine said that although there are differences in the various interpretations, there is truth in each. He prayed that the truth contained in each interpretation would give rise to peace among those who have different interpretations. He suggested that since several interpretations are true, Moses may have had all of these meanings in mind.

XII:32 Prayer for Understanding. Augustine affirmed that if Moses had only one meaning in mind when he wrote, that meaning should be considered the primary meaning, and so Augustine prayed for God's aid in interpreting the words of Moses.

COMMENTARY

The Influence of the Platonists. In speaking of the "heaven of heaven" (XII:2ff), the "formlessness of matter" (XII:4ff), the hierarchy of the creation (XII:7), and the belief that humans exist more as they turn to God and exist less as they turn away (XII:7), Augustine clearly revealed the Platonic influence in his understanding of creation. Though without any explicit reference to the Platonists, their influence flows like a strong undercurrent throughout Book XII, as he interpreted the biblical creation story through the lens of the Platonists. Any critical edition of *Confessions* contains multiple cross-references to the ideas of Porphyry and Plotinus, the Neoplatonists who greatly influenced Augustine's thinking.

How do you evaluate Augustine's claim that a passage of Scripture can have various levels of meaning?

Biblical Interpretation. In Book XII, Augustine gave his readers a fascinating look at his method of interpreting Scripture and a bit of his rationale for that method. Foundational to his approach was his assumption that the words of Scripture communicate on at least two levels, speaking both to the simple, who bring little of their own knowledge to Scripture, and to the learned, who bring an extensive background in the liberal arts. Far from seeing this possibility as a negative, Augustine saw in the multi-layered nature of the Scripture an indicator of God's intentional design.

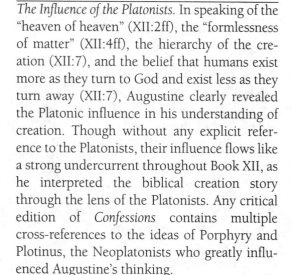

"If I Had Been Moses"

"So had I been Moses. . . I would have wished to be granted such skill in eloquence. . . that those unable to understand how God creates would not set aside the language as beyond their power to grasp; that those who had this ability and by reflection had attained to some true opinions would find in some terse words . . . that their true perceptions were not left out of account" (XII:26).

As a case study of the capability of biblical language to speak both to the simple and to those who wish to ponder its deeper mysteries, Book XII presents the words "heaven" and "earth" as examples. Here, the plain language communicates clearly enough to those who have little understanding. But, as Augustine explained, hidden beneath these simple words is a full understanding, namely that "heaven" refers to the invisible heaven where God dwells and that "earth" refers to visible creation, including the sky and the stars which are sometimes called "heaven."

Augustine responded to those who might suggest that any interpretation is false if it does not come from the simple, plain sense of the Scriptures, arguing that interpretations on two different levels are not only acceptable but also intended by God in order to allow His words to be easily grasped by beginners and at the same time propel the more learned readers into the Scripture's "wonderful profundity" (XII:14). Augustine went on to warn against the dangers of being scornful of Scripture because of its simplicity, likely recalling his own youthful rejection of the Bible because of its style.

Augustine made clear that because the Bible can be understood at different levels, a variety of interpretations can be understood as true. Using a set of his own foundations, he declared that he was open to any interpretation of the creation story that did not contradict these parameters and used the first few verses of Genesis to reveal a wide variety of acceptable interpretations. While recognizing the primary authority of the intent of Moses, Augustine spoke harshly against those who arrogantly assume they can infallibly declare the biblical writer's original intent.

Augustine's interpretive stance continues to be one of dependence on God's insight in order to obtain a true interpretation. With love for God and love for neighbor as the central principles

Stupid Interpretation

"See how stupid it is, among so large a mass of entirely correct interpretations . . . rashly to assert that a particular one has the best claim to Moses' view, and by destructive disputes to offend against charity itself . . ." (XII:25).

In what ways can Augustine be a model for us today as we interpret Scripture?

Prayer for Illumination

"Lord, we beg you to show us either what that one meaning is or some other true meaning of your choice . . . that we may feed on you and not be led astray by error" (XII:32).

for understanding the Scripture (XII:25), Augustine remained consistent with his God-directed posture throughout the rest of *Confessions*, looking to God as the final arbiter and the initiator in the revelation of God's truth.

BOOK XIII—FINDING THE CHURCH IN GENESIS

The Call of God

"With mounting frequency and by voices of many kinds you put pressure on me, so that from far off I heard and was converted and called upon you as you were calling to me" (XIII:1).

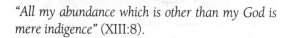

"All my abundance which is other than my God is mere indigence" (XIII:8).

BOOK-AT-A-GLANCE

1 Recalling Augustine's Own Re-creation

2–11 Understanding the Creator

12–34 Interpreting the Creation Story Allegorically

35–38 Returning to Rest

SUMMARY

Augustine gave an allegorical interpretation of Genesis 1, seeing in the various parts of the creation story images of God's creative work both in the church and in individual believers.

XIII:1 Conversion as Creation. Augustine recalled his own conversion in the language of the creation story, affirming that "it was good" and that at God's own initiative, Augustine was re-created by him "out of nothing."

XIII:2–4 God's Initiative in Creation and Conversion. Augustine continued on his theme of God's initiative, declaring that no part of the creation can claim any merit before God, who draws humans, bent toward darkness, to Himself. Interpreting the creation of light as "the spiritual creature" (XIII:3), he suggested a comparison between the darkness of the world as the darkness of the human condition and the darkness at the beginning of creation which remained to be converted to God. (XIII:4).

XIII:5–8 The Trinity in Creation. Augustine explicitly identified the Trinity in creation: "The Father who made these things; . . . the Son in whom he made these things" and the Spirit who "moved upon the waters." (XIII:5). He suggested that the Spirit was not mentioned until after the creation of the "heaven and earth" because there first had to be something (an abyss) over which he could be "borne above" (XIII:6). Augustine then made the human application, reflecting on those who are weighed down by evil desires "downwards to the steep abyss" but who are rescued by the love of the Holy Spirit who brings them "to the supereminent repose" where the Spirit is (XIII:7). He declared that just as all spiritual creation would have been held in the abyss apart from God's light, so, in the same way, it is impossible for any being less than God to provide itself with "a happy rest" (XIII:8).

XIII:9 The Holy Spirit. Augustine explained that though all three Persons of the Trinity are transcendent and "above" creation, only the Holy Spirit is described as being "above the waters," because only the Spirit is described as God's "gift" (Acts 2:38) to believers. Explaining that a body's weight causes it to move toward its proper place (fire, for example, moves up; a stone, down), Augustine affirmed that by God's gift of the Spirit, believers "are set on fire and carried upwards" (XIII:9).

Restlessness Revisited

"Things which are not in their intended position are restless" (XIII:9).

XIII:10 Creation and Time. Augustine explained that, though the story of creation appears through human eyes to move through successive steps in time, God actually created the formlessness of matter, gave the command "Let there be light," and elevated the Spirit above the abyss all at the same moment, "without an interval."

On the Trinity

"Who can understand the omnipotent Trinity? Yet everyone speaks about the subject, if indeed it can be the matter of discourse. It is a rare soul who knows what he is talking about when he is speaking of it" (XIII:11).

XIII:11 Unity and Diversity in the Trinity. Augustine described the persons of the Trinity in terms of being, knowing, and willing; but he warned his readers not to assume that this image allows them to comprehend the Unchangeable which is beyond them.

XIII:12 The Church in Creation. Augustine interpreted the creation of heaven and earth to refer to "the spiritual and carnal people of his church."

XIII:13–14 From Faith to Sight. Augustine laced together multiple allusions to Scripture (almost forty) in these brief sections to affirm that, though converted, the Christian still longs for what is yet to be. Most notably, he alluded to Paul, who said he "stretches out to those things which lie ahead," and to the psalmist, whose "soul thirsts for the living God," and to the bride who longs for the coming of the bridegroom (XIII:13).

"As the deer pants for streams of water, so my soul pants for you, O God" (Ps. 42:1).

XIII:15 The Firmament. Augustine interpreted the firmament allegorically to be referring to the Scripture. He refers to it as "a firmament of authority" which God has stretched over us. He acknowledged that those who dwell in heaven have no need to read the Scripture and that one day "the skin will be folded up." He affirmed that God's word is given through the Scripture "in the 'enigmatic obscurity' of clouds and through the 'mirror' of heaven" (Chadwick).

XIII:16–17 The Waters of Creation. After affirming that only God can know God as He is in Himself, (XIII:16), Augustine gave his twofold allegorical interpretation of the waters of creation. He referred to the bitter water in the sea as "the wicked desires of men's souls," around which God fixes limits. And he interpreted the fresh water to mean God's "sweet spring" by which the earth brings forth its fruit and souls yield works of mercy (XIII:17).

XIII:18 From Action to Contemplation. Augustine allegorically connected the fruit of the earth and the fruits of mercy grown in God's people. He suggested that believers can move from the "lower fruitfulness of action, arriving at the delightfulness of contemplation, obtaining the Word of Life above." Through our adhering to Scripture, Augustine suggested that God enables us to discern all things.

XIII:19 Dry Land. Augustine interpreted the appearance of dry land in the creation story as those souls who remove evil from their lives and do good.

XIII:20 Reptiles and Birds. In Augustine's view, the creation of reptiles and birds are representative of God's people who are at work in the midst of a world of temptations. Augustine explained that the extensive variety of symbols in his allegorical interpretation of Scripture speaks to the restlessness of the human heart.

XIII:21–23 The Living Soul. Augustine gave his interpretation of "the living soul," as baptized believers who are "separated from the bitterness of the waters" (XIII:21), who are created not like

On Scripture:

"For I know no other book so destructive of pride, so potent a weapon to crush your enemies and all who are on their guard against you, refusing to be reconciled with you and trying to justify the wrong they do. O Lord, I know no written words so pure as these, none that have induced me so firmly to make my confession to you, none that have so eased for me the task of bowing my neck to your yoke or so gently persuaded me to worship you for your sake and not for mine. Let me understand them, good Father. Grant me this gift, for I submit myself to them and it was for those who submit themselves that you made this solid shield" (XIII:15).

the animals "after its kind" but in the image of God, now having the capacity to be taught by God and made able to judge all things (XIII:22). But Augustine then enumerated those things that even the spiritual person should not judge, following quickly with a list of those areas where believers should exercise spiritual judgment (XIII:23).

XIII:24 Increase and Multiply. Augustine interpreted God's command to "increase and multiply" to refer allegorically to the presence of many true interpretations of the Scripture. Augustine went on to summarize the figurative meaning (which he said is the way he preferred to think Scripture is intended) found in Genesis 1.

XIII:25–26 Fruits of the Earth. Augustine referred back to his allegorical interpretation of "these fruits of the earth" as works of mercy, suggesting that ministers deserve to receive these acts of mercy in a special way. He affirmed that when acts of mercy are done, the fruit lies in the intention with which they were given rather than in the gift given (XIII:26).

XIII:27 Fishes and Whales. Augustine interpreted "fish and whales" to symbolize the miracle required to convert carnal men and infidels. Augustine asserted that when unbelievers do good works, they are not doing them out of holy and right intent. In so doing, they give the gift without the fruit.

XIII:28 Very Good. Augustine explained that the reason God seven times referred to the parts of His creation as "good," but on the eighth occasion referred to it as "very good" was because the whole of the creation was more beautiful than any of the constituent parts, just as the entire body is more beautiful than any individual part.

XIII:29 God and Time. Augustine considered why, when God is beyond time, the Scripture declares that God looked on each successive day and called His creation good. He responded that God is speaking to persons in time and so He uses language that is comprehensible in that context.

"And God saw all that He had made, and behold, it was very good" (Gen. 1:31, NASB).

XIII:30 Confusion of the Manichees. Augustine contrasted the biblical creation story with the confusion of the Manichees, who denied that God made everything out of nothing and who claim that many things in the world were created by a being that is different from and opposed to God.

XIII:31 The Goodness of Creation. Augustine declared that people only see God's goodness in creation through God's eyes. The Manichees saw creation as evil. Others see creation but not as coming from the Creator. Those see clearest who see creation with the help of the Spirit—through God's eyes.

XIII:32 Male and Female. Augustine listed the various parts of the creation which can be seen and then described the making of male and female, a distinction which parallels the two elements of the soul. One of these elements, the power of reasoning and understanding, is dominant, and the power of response or obedience is submissive.

XIII:33–34 Creation and Redemption. After praising God for His works of creation, Augustine began with an affirmation of God's predestined plan and retold the salvation story, weaving together the language of creation and the language of personal faith.

XIII:35–38 Eternal Rest. Augustine returned to the theme with which he began Book I: rest. He acknowledged that "this most goodly array of things very good" (XIII:35) will pass away because in the creation there is beginning and ending, "morning and evening." He went on to point out that the seventh day in the creation story is given no ending, no evening, a fact which he took to represent the never-ending Sabbath of eternal life. Augustine concluded by affirming that no person or angel can enable another to understand God's rest. That rest, Augustine affirmed, is only received by asking, seeking, and knocking.

COMMENTARY

The Transcendence of God. The creation story, for Augustine, served as a catalyst for his reflection on the radical distinction between God and His creatures (XIII:2). In describing the tendency of the creation to "move towards the chaos where there is no control" (XIII:2, Chadwick), Augustine spoke with a familiar Platonic accent, portraying the created order as a hierarchy that moves away from God toward formlessness. And in a similar way, he portrayed a fundamental distinction between humans who are drawn "downwards to the steep abyss" and the Spirit who lifts them up (XIII:7).

Creation out of Fullness

"You made [creation] not because you needed it, but from the fullness of your goodness" (XIII:4).

Augustine found in the creation story cause for repeated reflection on the initiative of God. After recalling his own dependence on God's recalling him even when he was bent toward darkness, he affirmed that those receiving the "light" owe this gift solely to God's goodness and grace (XIII:3).

From Creation to Redemption. Augustine repeatedly connected the story of creation's change from darkness to light to the human experience of conversion.

"For you were once darkness, but now you are light in the Lord" (Eph. 5:8).

Augustine began Book XIII with obvious echoes of his own conversion as he described the beginnings of creation as the "disordered flux of spiritual formlessness" of creation which "became converted." It is significant and consistent with his point of view throughout *Confessions* that his high-minded theological reflections move him to intensely personal responses. As he described the role of the Spirit in creation, his reflections ultimately led him to cry out, "My God, give me yourself . . ." (XIII:8), maintaining a consistent connection between the profound and the personal.

What biblical support could be offered for Augustine's claim that conversion is an action of creation?

Under the Word. Through his allegorical interpretation of the firmament, Augustine made clear his foundational assumption that the Scriptures are to be seen as "above" believers. It is this attitude toward Scripture that leads many churches to maintain a tradition of a high pulpit to remind congregations that God's word is "above" them, not an object of human investigation to be conveniently carried in a believer's back pocket. In Augustine's allegory, just as humans find themselves beneath the vast expanse of the sky, the magnitude of which they can never fathom, in the same way they are under God's word revealed in the Scriptures.

Creation in Us

"All these things we see, and they are very good, because you see them in us" (XIII:34).

Interpretation of Scripture. Augustine's essential interpretive assumption is to look beyond the literal words of the Scripture and to find symbols in those words that point to a deeper application for the believer. In this light Augustine suggested that God's command "be fruitful and multiply" points beyond its literal meaning to the multiplicity of fruitful meanings that can be found in a figurative treatment of the Scripture (XIII:24), an approach which he believes to be the most consistent with Scriptures' intent. Even though in Book XIII Augustine made no explicit reference to the influence of Ambrose, it is worth remembering that Ambrose's figurative approach to the Old Testament provided a crucial stepping-stone for Augustine's own conversion.

Spiritual Gifts. Augustine's allegory suggests an interesting hierarchy of spiritual gifts, as he refers to the sun as the gift of wisdom and the moon as the gift of knowledge. Augustine made clear that the gifts he interpreted as "stars" (gifts of faith, healing, miraculous powers, prophecy, discernment of spirits, tongues) are inferior to the gift of wisdom and are useful for those who are spiritually immature.

The Allegory in Outline. In Augustine's allegory, heaven and earth symbolize the spiritual and physical creations; light and darkness refer to "just and unjust souls" (XIII:24); the heaven and earth refer to "the spiritual and carnal members of his Church" (XIII:12); the firmament between the waters refers to Scripture; the sea refers to "the evil desires of souls" (XIII:17); the dry land refers to the "zeal of devoted souls" (XIII:24); reptiles and birds refer to God's ministers; fruit-bearing plants refer to works of mercy; lights in the heavens refer to spiritual gifts; and the living soul refers to baptized believers.

BIBLIOGRAPHY

LATIN TEXTS

1934—M. Skutella, Teubner of Leipzig (a critical edition of *Confessions* upon which a number of subsequent editions have depended, based primarily on ninth-century manuscripts)

1981—H. Juergens and W. Schaub, Teubner at Stuttgart (a revised version of Skutella's work)

1992—James J. O'Donnell, Clarendon Press at Oxford

ENGLISH TRANSLATIONS:

1620—Sir Tobie Matthew, courtier and diplomat

1631—William Watts, Rector of St. Alban's, Wood Street

1660—Abraham Woodhead, Catholic writer (first ten books)

1739—Bishop Challoner (first ten books)

1838—E. B . Pusey's revision of Watt's translation (This became the standard translation.)

1878—W. H. Hutchings (entirely new translation of first ten books)

1897—C. Bigg (entirely new translation of first nine books)

1961—R. S. Pine-Coffin, Penguin Books

1991—Henry Chadwick, Oxford University Press

1997—Maria Boulding, New City Press, Hyde Park, New York

SIGNIFICANT BOOKS

Bourke, Vernon J. *Augustine's Love of Wisdom: An Introspective Philosophy*. West Lafayette, IN: Purdue University Press, 1992.

———. *Augustine's Quest of Wisdom: His Life, Thought and Works*. Albany, NY: Magi Books, Inc., 1993.

———. *The Essential Augustine*. Indianapolis, IN: Hackett Publishing Co., 1974.

Brown, Peter. *Augustine of Hippo*. Berkeley: The University of California Press, 1967.

Miethe, Terry L. *Augustinian Bibliography, 1970–1980: With Essays on the Fundamentals of Augustinian Scholarship*. Westport, CT: 1982.

SHEPHERD'S NOTES

SHEPHERD'S NOTES